LIVING THE PSALMS

LIVING THE PSALMS

A Confidence for All Seasons

MAXIE DUNNAM

UPPER ROOM BOOKS

NASHVILLE

LIVING THE PSALMS

Cover Design: Jim Bateman
Book Design: Richard Cook
Cover Transparency: Bill Ross/Westlight
First Printing: November 1990 (15)
ISBN: 0-8358-0622-7
Library of Congress Catalog Card Number: 90-83523

Printed in the United States of America

T*o Randy,*
whose life and prayer
is a living psalm
and gives us a
confidence for all
seasons

CONTENTS

INTRODUCTION

*T*housands of books have been written on the Psalms. Why another? Only this: The Psalms never cease speaking to our hearts and minds. If one's vocation is communicating the "good news," as mine is, then we are almost always in the state of "I can't help it!"—"What we have seen and heard we declare to you" (I John 1:3, NEB).

It isn't that I have something new to say, only a desire to say it with an urgency and freshness so that, in the providence of God, someone reading this may find that which gives hope and life.

Then there is this very personal reason. At the time of this writing, my brother-in-law (my wife's only brother), Randy, is going through a long, hard, anguishing bout with cancer. Randy is forty-one and married, with two precious children, twelve and six years old. It's a family battle! In the summer of 1989, I preached a series of sermons on selected psalms. I sent some of the recorded messages to Randy. In response, he wrote letters of gratitude, letters that shared the depth of his struggle and his feelings. He told me about the spiritual direction he was receiving through a friend and how the Psalms had grown in meaning during his illness. "How I wish I had discovered them long ago!" was his poignant word. He urged me to continue to introduce others to this tremendous reservoir of guidance and strength.

So, in a sense, this book is my response to Randy, who in his battle has taught me and those who love him so much about faith, prayer, hope, perseverance, the healing power of humor, and love.

The Psalms are basically prayers—the prayers of the people of Israel. They are primarily community prayers, prayers for the people in worship. But the individual prayer is here as well. Though most of them were used in Israel's corporate worship, they reflect the deep cries of individuals.

What does prayer do for us? It helps us to reflect and to interiorize—to go inside, to dismiss the mood and direction of the masses and to seek our real, destined way. In prayer, we look for the meaning of daily events, and sometimes we are given the meaning, shocking though it may be.

A woman said to a guest at dinner, "We say grace at dinner each day to remind us around here that there is something bigger than our egos." Prayer can free us from the gravitational pull of our egos and remind us of the goodness and might of God. Prayer can move us from self-centered preoccupation to wonder and awe. It can bring into focus our pain and frustration and that of others, reminding us that we must share the burden of these pains and frustrations.

In a word, prayer brings us to God. It allows us to think God's thoughts after God, and it serves, with other spiritual disciplines, to conform us to the image of God's Son, Jesus.

Not only are the Psalms sources of prayer—they teach us. They teach us who God is and who we are in relation to God. The teaching derives from prayer, from the psalmists' honest confrontation with life situations in the experience of God.

That's the perspective of this book. It is teaching, but it is experiential teaching, teaching out of the prayer experience of the psalmists and out of our own experiences, which hopefully will become experience-prayer.

We are not studying the Psalms; we are allowing the Psalms to study us and to speak to us the things of God.

At the close of the book I have provided two sets of questions related to each chapter. One is for personal reflection. You will profit more and will allow the Psalms to study you and to speak to you the things of God if you will spend some time responding to those questions for personal reflection. Use a notebook and write down your responses and reflections.

Then there are questions for group discussion. Sharing this study with a group will be an exciting and enriching experience. Invite ten to twelve others to join you. Use each chapter as the study for a week and then gather as a group to share responses.

The questions for group discussion will provide more than enough guidance for an hour or an hour-and-a-half group gathering. The questions are deliberately personal, and your group sharing should focus there. If individuals will respond to the questions for personal reflection, they will come to the group with rich offerings for the shared life of the community.

One person might lead the group for the entire period, or a different discussion leader may be appointed for each meeting. The key is for the leaders to plan ahead. Look at the questions and decide which ones should receive primary attention because, chances are, you will not have time to cover them all. Also, stay sensitive to individual sharing. Be aware of the dynamic of ministry—people caring for one another.

This kind of study lends itself to spontaneous celebration and prayer. As a leader or a participant, don't hesitate to make suggestions such as, "I think we ought to sing a hymn of praise after that sharing of Nancy's—rejoicing with her in her experience," or, "I think we ought to pray right now for John. What he has shared is cause for us to lift him up in prayerful support." And, of course, be sensitive to other ways to respond in love and care to persons in the group who are sharing.

When you do this, the Psalms will become for your community what they have been for communities of faith across the centuries—resources to make real and celebrate God's presence among us.

God bless you as you allow these psalms to study you and to speak to you the things of God.

PSALM 30

I will extol thee, O LORD, for thou hast drawn me up,
  and hast not let me my foes rejoice over me.
O LORD my God, I cried to thee for help,
  and thou hast healed me.
O LORD, thou hast brought up my soul from Sheol,
  restored me to life from among those gone down to the Pit.

Sing praises to the LORD, O you his saints,
  and give thanks to his holy name.
For his anger is but for a moment,
  and his favor is for a lifetime.
Weeping may tarry for the night,
  but joy comes with the morning.

As for me, I said in my prosperity,
  "I shall never be moved."
By thy favor, O LORD,
  thou hadst established me as a strong mountain;
thou didst hide thy face,
  I was dismayed.

To thee, O LORD, I cried;
  and to the LORD I made supplication:
"What profit is there in my death,
  if I go down to the Pit?
Will the dust praise thee?
  Will it tell of thy faithfulness?

Hear, O LORD, and be gracious to me!
O LORD, be thou my helper!"
Thou hast turned for me my mourning into dancing;
   thou hast loosed my sackcloth
   and girded me with gladness,
that my soul may praise thee and not be silent.
   O LORD my God, I will give thanks to thee for ever.

PSALM 34

I will bless the LORD at all times;
   his praise shall continually be in my mouth.
My soul makes its boast in the LORD;
   let the afflicted hear and be glad.
O magnify the LORD with me,
   and let us exalt his name together!

I sought the LORD, and he answered me,
   and delivered me from all my fears.
Look to him, and be radiant;
   so your faces shall never be ashamed.
This poor man cried, and the LORD heard him,
   and saved him out of all his troubles.
The angel of the LORD encamps
   around those who fear him, and delivers them.
O taste and see that the LORD is good!
   Happy is the man who takes refuge in him!
O fear the LORD, you his saints,
   for those who fear him have no want!
The young lions suffer want and hunger;
   but those who seek the LORD lack no good thing.

Come, O sons, listen to me,
   I will teach you the fear of the LORD.
What man is there who desires life,
   and covets many days, that he may enjoy good?

Keep your tongue from evil,
  and your lips from speaking deceit.
Depart from evil, and do good;
  seek peace, and pursue it.
The eyes of the LORD are toward the righteous,
  and his ears toward their cry.
The face of the LORD is against evildoers,
  to cut off the remembrance of them from the earth.
When the righteous cry for help, the LORD hears,
  and delivers them out of all their troubles.
The LORD is near to the brokenhearted,
  and saves the crushed in spirit.

Many are the afflictions of the righteous;
  but the LORD delivers him out of them all.
He keeps all his bones;
  not one of them is broken.
Evil shall slay the wicked;
  and those who hate the righteous will be condemned.
The LORD redeems the life of his servants;
  none of those who take refuge in him will be condemned.

ONE

O TASTE AND SEE

*D*o you have a favorite psalm—
other than Psalm 23? Is there a psalm that has spoken to you in a
special way—encouraging, strengthening, supporting, comforting,
or healing you?

Karla Grant is a young mother in our church, a dynamic Christian. She's one of those persons who has the rare gift of joy, and the
expression of it is almost always on her face. When I think of her, I
am reminded of the words of a song, "Joy is the banner flying high
over the castle of my heart when the King is in residence there."

In a worship service at our church, Karla shared her witness—a
brief account of her Christian pilgrimage. Two verses from the
Psalms, one from Psalm 34, the other from Psalm 30, are the
linchpins which hold her life together.

This is her story. Six weeks after she and her husband, Don,
welcomed the first of their three children into the world in February 1977, they received the unhappy and frightening news that
Karla had melanoma. During that difficult time, Karla's mother
gave her a special verse to cling to, Psalm 34, verse 4: "I sought
the Lord, and he answered me, and delivered me from all my
fears."

Karla was admitted into the hospital on Good Friday for surgery
the next morning. But because there was controversy among the

pathologists about whether or not the tissue was malignant, she was released from the hospital on Saturday. She spent Easter at home, praising the Lord and thinking that everything was OK. Her joy was diminished on Monday morning when the doctor called and said he had changed his mind; he wanted to go ahead with the operation just to be sure. So, she checked back into the hospital and had the surgery. She prayed that the cancer would be contained in one small area without spreading. The surgery was successful, and the medical report revealed that there were no further malignant cells in the tissue.

After recounting these details, Karla shared a beautiful conviction: "I believe that I've experienced a miracle, and I'm more grateful than words can express. I don't understand why the Lord chooses to heal some people on earth while others must wait to receive their ultimate healing in heaven, but I take comfort in some words which I quote from Chuck Swindoll: 'God is too kind to ever be cruel, too wise to ever make a mistake, too deep to ever explain himself.' " Then she added, "I still claim Psalm 34:4 often as I face the various fears and doubts that Satan throws my way. But I would like to share with you another precious verse that I will use to praise Jesus for the rest of my life—Psalm 30:2: 'I cried to you for help, O Lord my God, and you healed me' " (TEV).

Karla closed her testimony with these words: "Knowing and praising God for what he has done in the past helps deliver us from fear and depression in the present."

How true!

In this chapter we look at the two psalms from which Karla drew her strength: Psalm 30 and Psalm 34. *Affirmation* is the theme of Psalm 30: "Weeping may tarry for the night, but joy comes with the morning" (30:5*b*). The *call* is the theme of Psalm 34: "O taste and see that the Lord is good!" (34:8*a*). That affirmation and call go together.

PSALM 30: JOY COMES IN THE MORNING

Let's look first at Psalm 30. Of this psalm *The Interpreter's Bible* says:

Although this psalm in Jewish ritual is used at the feast of
Dedication as a national song, it surely was entirely personal
to its original author. A man had been sick to death; he was
now well again, and he gave God the praise. Not only so, but
he also records the spiritual benefit obtained through a period of physical illness, giving a touch or two of intimate auto-
biography (Sclater, page 158).

The psalmist is reflecting; therefore, the sequence of events is
disjointed. If you change the order of the verses, the psalmist's
response to God and his praise have a movement which reaches a
crescendo of joy. Read it thus:

> As for me, I said in my prosperity,
>   "I shall never be moved."
> By thy favor, O Lord,
>   thou hadst established me as a strong mountain;
> thou didst hide thy face,
>   I was dismayed.
> To thee, O Lord, I cried;
>   and to the Lord I made supplication:
> "What profit is there in my death,
>   if I go down to the Pit?
> Will the dust praise thee?
>   Will it tell of thy faithfulness?
> Hear, O Lord, and be gracious to me!
>   O Lord, be thou my helper!"
> (verses 6-10)

> I will extol thee, O Lord, for thou hast drawn me up,
>   and hast not let my foes rejoice over me.
> O Lord my God, I cried to thee for help,
>   and thou hast healed me.
> O Lord, thou hast brought up my soul from Sheol,
>   restored me to life from among those gone down to the
>   Pit.
> (verses 1-3)

> Thou hast turned for me my mourning into dancing;
>   thou hast loosed my sackcloth
>   and girded me with gladness,

19

that my soul may praise thee and not be silent.
O Lord my God, I will give thanks to thee for ever.
(verses 11-12)

Sing praises to the Lord, O you his saints,
    and give thanks to his holy name.
For his anger is but for a moment,
    and his favor is for a lifetime.
Weeping may tarry for the night,
    but joy comes with the morning.
(verses 4-5)

What a witness! What a testimony of commitment and trust! Let's look at it. In this new order, the movement of the psalm may be thus: *Problem, Plea, Praise,* and *Promise.*

The Problem

The psalmist has recovered from a grave illness. He had been sick to death, and he is praising God for deliverance. But there's something else going on. There's a problem behind the problem: moral failure. In verse 6, he says, "As for me, I said in my prosperity, 'I shall never be moved.' "

Here is our common sin: We think we're sufficient unto ourselves. It is the *illusion* of prosperity: "I said in my prosperity, 'I shall never be moved.' "

The psalmist was aware that God had given him his well-being. Verse 7 says, "By thy favor, O Lord, thou hadst established me as a strong mountain."

Then it happened; the bottom fell out. Everything was going well: There was money in the bank, a condominium at the beach, dinner at the country club every Friday, and lunch at the University Club on Sunday. The children were in the best private schools, there were two or three cars in the garage, and Nautilus workouts three times and/or tennis twice weekly at the racquet club. When he had "the world by the tail," it happened: "Thou didst hide thy face, I was dismayed" (verse 7).

It happened, and happens, in a lot of different ways. A heart attack reminds us of the stress we were under trying to keep up the good life. Cancer wraps its terrible clutches around our spouse, and we become aware of how fragile life is, how meaningless the accoutrements of prosperity are, and how precious the love of husband and wife is. A son or a daughter goes to the depths of rebellion. A spouse or child becomes drug dependent, and we are willing to give every penny we have to make him or her whole again.

All of a sudden it becomes clear to us. What we have given so much energy to, what we have thought was so important, what we have put our security and our hopes in—all of a sudden begins to fade or even crumble. "Thou didst hide thy face, I was dismayed."

The point is not hard to get; the problem is not difficult to identify. Before he was struck down, the psalmist was at ease and all was well. But his sense of security led to a false confidence: "I shall never be moved."

It wasn't that the psalmist didn't trust in God. He confessed his trust: "By thy favor, O Lord, thou hadst established me as a strong mountain." But he took God for granted; he didn't reckon with "the fact that the Lord might withdraw from him because of his sins, known or unknown, or because of reasons known only to God himself" (Sclater, page 161).

So, when the psalmist felt the Lord had withdrawn from him, he was dismayed. In English, the word *dismayed* is an understatement. The psalmist was flabbergasted, shattered; he felt his life was going to pieces.

Notice that the problem was twofold sin: the sin of having his security in the wrong place and the sin of presumption—presuming that God would always be blessing him. He failed to keep close scrutiny on his loyalties and commitments; he failed to recognize the falseness of his self-sufficiency and self-centeredness.

The Plea

Now look at the *plea:* "To Thee, O Lord, I cried; and to the Lord I made supplication" (verse 8).

Note this first: It's hard to know God unless you know your need of God. That goes back to the problem. The psalmist thought he was secure, established as a "strong mountain." He didn't think he needed God.

Sometimes we feel as if we don't need God. It's not that God has let us down or that God has made us angry; it's simply that we don't sense within ourselves a need for God's presence and participation in our lives.

Human relationships work the same way. The people with whom we open up our lives and share the intimacies of our hearts are those people we feel a strong need for, and we know that they have a reciprocal need for us. Now and then, we are introduced to a person who impresses us. Our instincts tell us that this is a special person we might want to know better. But has it happened to you as it has to me? Sometimes, the person I want to know better doesn't seem to want to know me. So there is no getting to know each other better. If there is no mutual need and desire to know each other, then two people do not become close.

The same thing is true in our relationship to God: It's hard to know God unless you know your need of God.

But the plea of the psalmist teaches us something else. There is a radical suggestion implicit in this plea: Not only is our relationship to God of value to us, it is of value to God. Give attention to this bold, argumentative prayer from verse 9:

> What profit is there in my death,
>   if I go down to the Pit?
> Will the dust praise thee?
>   Will it tell of thy faithfulness?

Put in our vernacular, it may sound like this: "Lord, what good is it going to do you if I die and go to hell? Will my rotting body offer any praise to you? Will the fact that I'm lost give any sort of witness to the fact that you are a faithful God? that the good work that you began in me is going to be completed? that you are a persevering God who is not willing that any of your children be lost? What good is going to come to you if I'm lost?"

Let me share a personal experience with this part of the psalm and a vision that came to me through it.

As I write this, the most significant person in my faith journey, David McKeithen, is dying of a raging brain tumor. Fortunately, I had the opportunity to visit with him recently while he was still able to communicate. The two days with him were sad, but joyful; painful, but healing.

The six weeks prior to my visit had been especially tough for me. It seemed as though everything was happening at once: emotionally wrenching pastoral involvements including the accidental death of a thirteen-year-old; the death of one of my dearest friends, Tom Carruth; a huge responsibility for an event for the World Methodist Council; and in the midst of it all, a week-long, very painful physical problem. I was stressed out as much as I have ever been.

And now, David's impending death.

David brought me into The Methodist Church. Under his ministry I answered the call to preach. He married Jerry and me and has baptized and married some of our children. Our lives have been woven together in so many ways.

My visit was a painful time. I cried a lot—and I didn't sleep much. Early one morning, about five o'clock, unable to sleep, I slipped out on the patio and began to pray—to relive my relationship with David and to recall my faith journey that he has been such a part of. When there was enough light, I began to read the Psalms—rather randomly.

Somehow I got to Psalm 30. This remarkable word of praise grabbed my attention: "Thou hast turned for me my mourning into dancing; thou hast loosed my sackcloth and girded me with gladness, that my soul may praise thee and not be silent" (verses 11 and 12). Then there was my favorite line in all the Psalms: "Weeping may tarry for the night, but joy comes with the morning" (verse 5).

All of that was good for my soul . . . but that was not the fresh vision that lifted me. The fresh vision came from that plea from the psalmist. As he faced his own death, he argued boldly with God in verse 9: "What profit is there in my death, if I go down to the Pit? Will the dust praise thee? Will it tell of thy faithfulness?"

I had what first felt like an irreverent thought: What would God have done without David McKeithen? I was not only thinking of what David had meant to me, but of the countless people who had come to Christ and tasted of the kingdom through him.

I realized that not only is our relationship to God of value to us, it is of value to God. *There is a place in the heart of God that only I can fill.* Wow! Think of it. There is a place in the heart of God that only you can fill.

Late that afternoon after my experience with Psalm 30, we were all in the room with David: Marguerite, his precious wife—one of God's great women, his two sons—both United Methodist ministers, and Jerry and me. It just seemed right that we worship together. I read from 1 Thessalonians, chapter 5, the passage about Jesus' second coming and our resurrection with him. We prayed and sang hymns. I told the group about my reflections on the psalm and how the thought had come, What would God have done without David McKeithen? Never having lost his sense of humor, David, who could talk very little, spoke up and said, "Oh, I think he might have made it OK."

Well, maybe—but maybe not. In my weakness, pain, and stress, the vision had come. There's a place in God's heart that only I can fill—a place that only you can fill. That's the reason I said earlier that my time with David was sad, but joyful; painful, but healing. The Lord works that way.

Augustine said, "Thou hast made us for Thyself, and our hearts are restless till they rest in Thee."

But here is the question the psalmist's plea calls us to ponder: Could it be true that there is a place in God's heart that only *you* can fill, that only *I* can fill—that *God* is restless until we rest in him?

What a thought—that there is a place in God's heart that only you can fill! That's more than a thought; it's a truth verified in the most dramatic and convincing way: "For God so loved the world, that he gave his only begotten Son, that whosoever believeth in him should not perish, but have everlasting life" (John 3:16, KJV).

Think about that for a moment. I don't know a more exhilarating truth. If you love someone, you need that someone to return that love, don't you? Sure you do! So it is with God. God loves you and needs your love. God will not allow death to destroy you. If you are forever separated from God, it will be your choice, not God's. In God's heart there is a place that only you can fill.

The Praise

That leads to the next part: *praise.*

> Thou hast turned for me my mourning into dancing;
>> thou hast loosed my sackcloth
>> and girded me with gladness,
> that my soul may praise thee and not be silent.
>> (Psalm 30:11-12)

There's nothing like it in all of literature. As one old preacher said, "If Shakespeare had written that, we should not have heard the end of it."

The psalmist gives God the credit for working in his life in such a dramatic way. The psalmist pledges to praise and thank God forever and ever.

The Promise

Now the crescendo of joy—the *promise* which is at the heart of the psalmist's praise:

> For his anger is but for a moment,
>> and his favor is for a lifetime.
> Weeping may tarry for the night,
>> but joy comes with the morning.
>> (Psalm 30:5)

I don't have a single favorite psalm, but I think this is my favorite line in all of them: "Weeping may tarry for the night, but joy comes with the morning." That says it all—no commentary is needed—but maybe a story will penetrate the truth to our hearts.

Somewhere I read of a young man whose wife had died, leaving him with a small son. Back home from the cemetery on the day of the funeral, he and his son went to bed early because, in his sorrow, the young widower could think of nothing else he could bear to do. As he lay there in the darkness, grief-stricken, numb with sorrow, the little boy broke the spell from his little bed with a disturbing question: "Daddy, where is Mommy?"

The young father tried to answer the boy and tried to get him to go to sleep, but the question kept coming from his confused, childish mind. "Where is Mommy? When is she coming home?"

After a while the father got up and brought the little boy to bed with him. But the child was still disturbed and restless, persistently asking his probing, heartbreaking questions.

Finally the little boy reached out his hand through the darkness and placed it on his father's face, asking, "Daddy, is your face towards me?" Given assurance, both verbally and by his own touch, that his father's face was indeed toward him, the little boy said, "If your face is toward me, I think I can go to sleep." And in a little while, he was quiet.

The father lay there in the darkness and in childlike faith prayed, "O God, the way is dark and I confess that I do not see my way through right now, but if your face is toward me, somehow I think I can make it."

We can make it if God's face is toward us—and certainly that's the case. God's face is always toward us. Weeping may tarry for the night, but joy comes with the morning.

PSALM 34: O TASTE AND SEE

In Psalm 30, we read the *affirmation*; now we read the *call*: "O taste and see that the Lord is good!" (Psalm 34:8a). The line that follows this call is another telling affirmation that completes verse 8: "Happy is the man who takes refuge in him!"

This psalm could well be the theme of the entire psalter. It is certainly the core experience of the person of faith.

Psalm 34 is a psalm of witness, a "show-and-tell" testimony: "O taste and see that the Lord is good!" How do you know? You ask the psalmist, and he responds by telling you and showing you how it has been in his own life.

In verses 4 through 7, the psalmist enumerates what good God has done for him:

God answered me.

God delivered me from all my fears.

God heard me and saved me out of my troubles.

That is the show-and-tell personal witness of the psalmist. But he doesn't stop there. Before he closes, he enumerates again the signs of the goodness of God.

> When the righteous cry for help, the Lord hears,
> and delivers them out of all their troubles.
> The Lord is near to the broken-hearted,
> and saves the crushed in spirit.
> Many are the afflictions of the righteous;
> but the Lord delivers him out of them all.
>
> (Psalm 34:17-19)

God Is Good

There are two monumental truths expressed in this psalm. The first is the most obvious, for it is the theme: God is good. That is what the psalm is about. It begins as a song of personal praise: "I will bless the Lord at all times; his praise shall continually be in my mouth"(verse 1).

The psalm is a personal witness to the goodness of God; yet it goes beyond the personal and seeks to draw others into the experience. Thus it is an invitation—a call to others to "taste and see that the Lord is good."

Let's take a brief detour now to consider an incidental but important truth related to the idea of invitation. The depth of our religious experience can be tested by the irrepressible impulse to share with others what we have experienced—to bring others to the fountain from which we have drunk. That's what evangelism is all about. Asian theologian D. T. Niles defined it as "one beggar telling another beggar where to find bread." The strategy for evangelism rests on this simple foundation: personal witness. One loving heart sets another heart on fire; one person whose spiritual hunger and thirst has been satisfied introduces another to him who alone will feed our ravaging hunger—Jesus, "the bread which came down from heaven" (John 6:41). Who will assuage our burning thirst? Jesus, the living water "welling up to eternal life" (John 4:14).

Do you feel an irrepressible impulse to share your Christian experience, to bring others to the fountain from which you have drunk? Keep asking yourself that question. It's a good way to test the growing depth of your relationship to Christ.

27

Now back to the central truth we are underscoring—the goodness of God. Have you seen the magnificent movie *The Color Purple?* It authenticates the movie medium as a powerful tool for social commentary and criticism as well as a legitimate art form. The book on which the movie is based is a collection of letters, some from Celie to God and some between Celie and her sister, Nettie. In one letter to Nettie, Celie tells about a conversation she and Shug had about God. Celie complains that God has never done much for her; her life has just been a chaos of suffering; her prayers don't seem to be answered; she just cannot relate to God anymore.

Shug asks Celie what her God looks like. "He big and old and tall and graybearded and white. He wear white robes and go barefooted." They agree that the God of Celie's imagination is just the God they've been taught to believe in. They go on to try to find some other way to describe what God is to them. Shug puts it this way:

> Here's the thing. . . . The thing I believe. God is inside you and inside everybody else. You come into the world with God. But only them that search for it inside find it. And sometimes it just manifest itself even if you not looking, or don't know what you looking for. Trouble do it for most folks, I think. Sorrow, lord. . . . God love everything you love—and a mess of stuff you don't. But more than anything else, God love admiration. . . . People think pleasing God is all God care about. But any fool living in the world can see it always trying to please us back. . . . always making little surprises and springing them on us when us least expect (Walker, pp. 200-204).

In other words, Shug was saying, "O taste and see that the Lord is good."

God Is Our Refuge

The second monumental truth in this psalm is this: God's goodness is not an escape from pain and suffering but a refuge of strength in the midst of it.

The psalmist makes no effort to evade reality. This is no "let-me-get-away-from it-all-and-find-relief" stance. The psalmist was

no stranger to fear and trouble. That's why the witness is so powerful. "Let the afflicted hear and be glad," he says. The Lord will not
leave you alone in your affliction.

Troubles do come. If yours haven't come yet, they will. But
the Lord delivers. That's the faith we hold to. Sometimes it's not
easy to hold to—but hold to it we must. Those who have experienced affliction, as the psalmist had, are credible witnesses.
Here is a contemporary witness—a letter to me which came
from a friend some time ago. I found it in a file where I keep
precious things.

> I went to the [ministers'] retreat not long ago. I never go
> each year without thinking of the time you were there with us.
> The theme was, appropriately, "Resources for Coping." I
> received warmth, love, and blessing after blessing as I talked
> with my sisters and brothers about some of the hard realities
> of life and the constant joy of God. I shared with the group
> what a year this had been for me. First, Brian's tragic acci-
> dent, my brother had two cancer operations (he is 29), my try-
> ing to take a study leave and work, getting mono this summer
> during my "vacation," then our marital difficulties. But
> through it all I have come to experience the growing power
> and meaning of Christian community as I have been nur-
> tured, and have seen all the members of my family supported,
> including [my wife].
>
> While it has been tough to face, I feel more accepting of
> the situation and that we are all coping well. I'd like to sit
> and talk for longer, but this short note will have to suffice. I
> know you care, and I wanted to share a little of what is hap-
> pening and mostly that things are okay. I am still hopeful,
> and with all the strength and resources, literally, that God has
> given me, I am trying to remain sensitive, loving, forgiving,
> and accepting of all those in my life who mean so much to
> me.

My friend could have added the invitation of the psalmist: "O
taste and see that the Lord is good." God's goodness is not an
escape from pain and suffering; rather, it is a refuge of strength in
the midst of it.

Early in the psalm, the writer says, "Look to him, and be radiant" (verse 5a), and he closes with this word, "The Lord redeems the life of his servants; none of those who take refuge in him will be condemned" (verse 22).

Remember the call of Psalm 34 and the affirmation of Psalm 30—"Weeping may tarry for the night, but joy comes with the morning" (Psalm 30:5b) and "O taste and see that the Lord is good!" (Psalm 34:8).

PSALM 4

Answer me when I call, O God of my right!
Thou hast given me room when I was in distress.
Be gracious to me, and hear my prayer.

O men, how long shall my honor suffer shame?
   How long will you love vain words, and seek after lies?   *Selah*
But know that the LORD has set apart the godly for himself;
   the LORD hears when I call to him.

Be angry, but sin not;
   commune with your own hearts
      on your beds, and be silent.   *Selah*

Offer right sacrifices,
   and put your trust in the LORD.

There are many who say, "O that we might see some good!
   Lift up the light of thy countenance upon us, O LORD!"
Thou hast put more joy in my heart
   than they have when their grain and wine abound.

In peace I will both lie down and sleep;
   for thou alone, O LORD, makest me dwell in safety.

PSALM 11

In the LORD I take refuge; how can you say to me,
    "Flee like a bird to the mountains;
for lo, the wicked bend the bow,
    they have fitted their arrow to the string,
    to shoot in the dark at the upright in heart;
if the foundations are destroyed,
    what can the righteous do"?

The LORD is in his holy temple,
    the LORD's throne is in heaven;
    his eyes behold, his eyelids test, the children of men.
The LORD tests the righteous and the wicked,
    and his soul hates him that loves violence.
On the wicked he will rain coals of fire and brimstone;
    a scorching wind shall be the portion of their cup.
For the LORD is righteous, he loves righteous deeds;
    the upright shall behold his face.

TWO

WHEN YOU FEEL TRAPPED

*C*laustrophobia is the fear of being closed in, trapped in a small space. It is a common phobia. Many of us experience it to varying degrees. I get a hint of it when I'm in an overcrowded elevator. Hardly ever am I in that situation without a question striking a bit of terror in my heart: What if this thing gets stuck?

Yet, the feeling of being trapped comes in areas of our lives that have nothing to do with feeling claustrophobic in small or closed-in spaces. There are many ways we can feel trapped.

Some of us feel trapped in jobs that have become drudgery; trapped in marriages where love has died and where neither partner is willing to take the radical steps and to expend the energy demanded to breathe life into the lifeless relationship; trapped at home with ill and aged parents who demand constant care; trapped at a point in mid-life when we feel we are losing our grip on reality and are responding irrationally to marriage and family and job—we call it mid-life crisis; trapped in the economic strictures of businesses that have failed or investments that have plummeted.

The catalogue of entrapment situations and circumstances is nearly endless. Perhaps it is not even a specific situation, just a feeling we have, expressed in the vernacular of Perry County,

Mississippi, where I'm from: "I'm damned if I do, and damned if I don't."

Columnist Art Buchwald began an article with this news bit:

> In Concord, California, a customer became enraged at an automated teller and kept punching it because the machine refused to dispense $80 from the man's account. The customer was arrested and charged with "malicious mischief."
>
> This is not an isolated incident. According to police reports, so many people are beating up on automated machines that it has become this nation's most serious crime problem (Buchwald, p. A-9).

With his typically sharp wit, Buchwald went on to write about the frustration of people who don't get what they look for from vending machines.

Does it make you mad? I've seen people livid with anger, pounding pay phones with their fists or kicking Coke machines mercilessly. At a truck stop once, I was waiting to use the telephone, and I saw a man literally pull the receiver out from the phone and throw it in the trash because he didn't get a coin return.

I see this kind of behavior as just one expression of the frustration that drives us to the point of wanting to throw up our hands in a despairing "what's the use!" It isn't just a matter of feeling cheated by a machine that you can't reason with—that's just the straw that breaks the camel's back. The problem is far larger, more complex, more common, and certainly more painful than it appears to be. It's the problem of life becoming too much, burdens weighing upon us, questions pressing for answers, responsibilities so great we don't feel adequate, and persons demanding of us more than we can give.

We get to the point where kicking a machine is the most innocent expression of our frustration and despair. Alone, we may throw up our hands and scream, or at least we may want to. Instead we keep the emotion bottled up until it bursts out in more unhealthy ways. We end up damaging other people rather than bruising our fists or scuffing our shoes when we attack a machine.

The experience of feeling trapped usually generates another strong feeling: We fantasize about moving to the country, or more romantically, to some tropical island yet undiscovered by civilization. Or we think about how it would be if we weren't married; if we didn't have the responsibility of children; if we were independently wealthy and didn't have to put up with all the emotional pressure and garbage that comes, sometimes, with making a living. You know what I'm talking about—all those pressures that make you want to run away, to drop out, to escape, to call it quits. In extreme cases, these pressures drive persons to literally drop out and seek alternative lifestyles, to leave their families and run, or most extremely, to commit suicide.

Many of us not only live *with* this fear, we live *in* it a substantial part of our lives. Each one of us gives battle to the thought of being left where we are, who we are, with no way out. The poet, Kenneth Patchen, expressed it this way:

> Isn't all our dread a dread of being
> Just here? Of being only this?
> Of having no other thing to become?
> Of having no where to go really
> But where we are?
>
> (Patchen, p. 328)

PSALM 4: THOU HAST GIVEN ME ROOM

The first verse of Psalm 4 speaks to the emotional onslaught of feeling trapped and wanting to run away:

> Answer me when I call, O God of my right!
> Thou hast given me room when I was in distress.
> Be gracious to me, and hear my prayer.
>
> (Psalm 4:1)

The line that speaks to the feeling of being trapped is the middle one: "Thou hast given me room when I was in distress."

David Allan Hubbard, President of Fuller Theological Seminary, reflects on the psalmist's situation in Psalm 4:

Were we to sit down and chat with the psalmist who gave us Psalm 4 . . . we might say to him, "Sir, you were obviously in deep trouble, trouble of mind and spirit, when you prayed to God your prayer that he was pleased to preserve in the Holy Scriptures. Your problems seemed pressing, yet your confidence in God remained strong. You seemed to come through the difficulty with your faith and devotion unscathed. How did you do it? What advice can you give me?"

"Well," the psalmist might reply, "the first thing you must do is face your problem. In my case, people were actually mocking my faith, claiming that it did no good to trust God in a time of drought. The crops were threatened; the livelihood of the land was in jeopardy. And I insisted that we must continue to pray to God for help. He alone could send the good rain we needed. It was this rain that people were praying for in the short prayer that I quoted in the psalm: 'There are many who say, O that we might see some good!' (v. 6).

"This good that they wanted to see was actually rain. When it did not come in time, they were frustrated. Many were tempted to look to a pagan god like Baal, the Canaanite fertility god. When I insisted that the Lord of the creation and exodus, the God of Abraham and Moses, was the only One who could help, they turned on me with bitter and harsh attacks.

"And I had to face my problem and take it to God. If I had tried to avoid it, it would not have gone away. It might have grown even more painful, and besides, if I run from my problems, how do I bring them to God for help?" (Hubbard, pp. 12-13).

Face the Problem

So that's a good starting place when we feel trapped. If we're going to find "room when in distress," we must honestly face our problems.

There are three specific truths we need to recognize as we think about facing our problems honestly:

• Problems do not go away by avoiding them.

• Rather, the opposite is true. When we try to avoid problems, they grow inside us; they are magnified.

• If we do not acknowledge and face our problems, we never come to the point of bringing those problems to God and receiving God's help.

I have a marvelous witness of this in a letter I received from a member of our congregation. I asked her permission to share this letter, and she was excited about the possibility that her witness may open the door for someone else.

Dear Maxie:

I have wanted to write to you since the third week of immersing myself in your book, *The Workbook on Spiritual Disciplines.* The first week was so full of little miracles that I was too frightened to accept that God was truly speaking to me. I was not comfortable. I now think that I felt too unworthy to receive such unconditional love. I also felt your own love pouring through the pages and heard your own voice. For that, I felt comfortable and grateful; the experiences were believable. The pivotal point occurred on day five of that crucial week three.

Parenthetically, on that day in the workbook the theme is "Naming the Demon" as a part of our confession. The dynamic focused on is that there is healing and redemptive power inherent in the naming process. It is the same principle as we are talking about here—acknowledging and facing our problems. My friend continues her letter:

I had spent many sleepless hours praying, actually begging for the recovery of our son. I read about your dilemma relating to your son, Kevin. You used words like these: . . . "anguishing . . . impatient . . . temper . . . perception blurred . . . escape . . . indulgent . . . self-condemnation . . . guilt of failure . . . FEAR."

The words that named my problems came to me easily: suffocating indulgence . . . fear . . . selfishness . . . anger . . . inconsistency . . . guilt . . . ALCOHOL. Nobody could have convinced me of the power of alcohol—ever. I was stuck in a dark basement of moral decay. There was no hope for me—all my pleading was for my son. The revelation was so obvious that I felt foolish . . . insane. It was not a "cop-out," but the truth. I had named the demon, and that demon was alcohol. I admitted that I was powerless and that my life had become unmanageable. Only God could restore me to sanity. These simple sentences made sense at last. I was given the second and first steps in that order.

The resistance of the apostles who were constant companions of Jesus reassured me. Trust. Faith. I quit begging and asked, as God instructed. Now I ask for guidance throughout the day and night—not just for my son or for me or for my family but for everyone whose "path intersects mine." I am grateful. Shame has been replaced by acceptance. I am eager to integrate the suffering into my life and use it as God would have me to.

My friend has learned the lesson of the psalmist: Face your problem. We must learn:

That problems do not go away by avoiding them.

Rather, the opposite is true—when we try to avoid problems, they are magnified and grow inside us.

If we do not acknowledge our problems, we never come to the point of bringing those problems to God and receiving God's help.

Grow in Prayer

The psalmist gives us a second direction when we feel trapped: Keep a prayer life going and growing. He puts it in a cryptic way in verses 3 and 4:

> But know that the Lord has set apart the godly for himself;
>> the Lord hears when I call to him.
> Be angry, but sin not;
>> commune with your own hearts on your beds, and be
>> silent.
>
> (Psalm 4:3-4)

Let me briefly underscore two crucial factors to which we give little thought when we talk about prayer. One, there are some things God cannot give a person until that person has prepared and proven his or her spirit by persistent prayer. As Henry Emerson Fosdick reminds us, "Such praying cleans the house, cleanses the windows, hangs the curtains, sets the table, opens the door, until God says, 'Lo! The house is ready. Now may the guest come in' " (Fosdick, p. 240).

Verse 4 of Psalm 4 says, "Commune with your own hearts on your beds, and be silent." The second factor is that we must face ourselves in prayer. Prayer that the psalmist teaches us about is "conferencing with ourselves." Is that a strange way to put it? Maybe the quaintness of the phrase will cause you to remember it: *conferencing* with yourself. Many of us use prayer as an escape from ourselves rather than an honest facing of self. In prayer we need to face ourselves as we come to God.

One of the greatest orthodox teachers of prayer, Bishop Theophan the Recluse, described the aim of Christian prayer in this fashion: "The principal thing is to stand, with the mind in the heart before God, and to go on standing before him unceasingly day and night, until the end of life."

That was a new image for me when I read it: to stand before God "with the mind in the heart." It means that we are to focus, to center our attention, to bring the thoughts and reflections of our minds to the core of our beings, to our hearts. We do not come to God with our feelings here, our thoughts there, our longings hither, and our fleshly and emotional passions yonder. We come as one integrated—our total being drawn as steel to a magnet into the spheres of our hearts, to our center where the Spirit meets us.

When we come to God in this fashion, confession is then translated into transformation. We have set the stage for change. Fritz Kunkel, in his book *In Search of Maturity*, makes the point clearly:

> Expression of what we find within ourselves, honest and reckless expression before the face of the Eternal, assuming responsibility for what we are, even if we are unaware of it, and asking God to help us to master the wild horses, or to revive the skeletons of horses which we dig out during the long hours of our confessions—this is the psychological method of religious self-education. It is a way of bringing to consciousness our unconscious contents, and of establishing control over our hidden powers. It is the way to mature responsibility. It is the old way of the Psalmist. "Yet who can detect his lapses? Absolve me from my faults unknown! And

hold thy servant back from willful sins, from giving way to them" (Psalm 19:12-13, Moffatt).

Not in the presence of a minister or a psychologist, but in the presence of God, things change completely. If you hate your brother, and you pour out all your hatred, remembering at the same time, as much as you can, the presence of God—and your hatred does not change, then you are not sufficiently aware either of the presence of God or of your hatred, and probably of neither. Be more honest, give vent to your emotions. You hate your brother; imagine his presence, before God tell him how you feel, kick him, scratch him. You are ten years old now—get up from your chair, don't pretend to be a wise old Buddha, pace the floor, yell, scream, punch the furniture, express yourself. Rant and rage until you are exhausted, or until you laugh at yourself (Kunkel, pp. 253-254).

You may think that extreme. Let it fit your own personality, your own style, but don't miss the point—conference with yourself. "Commune with your own hearts on your beds, and be silent."

Not only do we need guidance when we feel trapped, we need counsel when we want to run away. It's found in Psalm 11.

PSALM 11: IN THE LORD I TAKE REFUGE

Charles Simeon gave Psalm 11 the title "The Song of the Steadfast." There was a time when most preachers and Bible teachers accredited all the Psalms to David. Charles Simeon was one of these. C. H. Spurgeon records him saying:

David, at the different periods of his life, was placed in almost every situation in which a believer, whether rich or poor, can be placed; and in these heavenly compositions he delineates all the workings of the heart. He introduces, too, the sentiments and conduct of the various persons who were accessory either to his troubles or his joys; and thus sets before us a compendium of all that is passing in the hearts of men throughout the world. When he penned this Psalm he was under persecution from Saul, who sought his life, and hunted him "as a partridge upon the mountains." His timid friends were alarmed for his safety, and recommended him to flee to some mountain where he had a hiding-place, and thus to conceal himself from the rage of Saul. But David, being strong in faith, spurned the idea of resorting to any such pusillanimous expedients, and determined confidently to repose his trust in God (Spurgeon, p. 10).

Most Bible scholars now contend that the Psalms come from many sources, some from David to be sure, but most out of the faithful life of God's covenant people.

> According to L. Alonso Schökel the setting of [Psalm 11] is the temple. A persecuted innocent man flees to God's house and invokes the right of asylum. The temple employees inform him that the temple does not provide absolutely certain asylum. They advise him, therefore, to flee to the mountains like a bird (v 1). He reacts to such advice by professing his unshakeable confidence in the judgment of Yahweh (vv 4-7). When the foundations of public order are overthrown (v 3), the ultimate hope of justice resides with Yahweh (Craghan, pp. 51-52).

This person could well have been David. Some think it was David's reflection on the eve of Absalom's conspiracy, while others think it was at the height of Saul's persecution. Either could have been the case. In both settings David was surrounded by stealthy hostility. His friends and his own prudence counseled him to flee. Whether written by David or some other, Psalm 11 has affinity with what are called the "persecution psalms" (including Psalms 3, 7, 9, 14, and 17).

The psalm begins with a magnificent utterance of faith: "In the Lord I take refuge." It was the psalmist's answer to those who wanted him to run away. Those who wanted him to run away had a good argument. Look at verses 2 and 3:

> "For lo, the wicked bend the bow,
>   they have fitted their arrow to the string,
>   to shoot in the dark at the upright in heart;

> if the foundations are destroyed,
>   what can the righteous do"?
>   (Psalm 11:2-3)

The psalmist's answer was to trust in the Lord. That's good advice when we want to run away. It's the same guidance we find in Psalm 4 when we feel trapped. Look at verse 8 of Psalm 4: "In peace I will both lie down and sleep; for thou alone, O Lord, makest me dwell in safety."

Believe in the Presence of God

How could the psalmist sleep in peace? He trusted the Lord. He could trust the Lord for two reasons. One, he remembered the past acts of God. That's the way he began his psalm: "Thou hast given me room when I was in distress" (4:1). If you want to put it in our vernacular, God had always come through for him.

Roger Watson, a member of our church, has written a gospel song based on a prayer he heard an old man pray long ago. The lyrics are, "Lord, we know what you gonna do, 'cause we see what you've already done."

Test that in your own experience. Have you experienced God at work in your life in a particular way? in the life of someone else? How long ago was the experience you now recall? What does how long ago the experience was say about your trust in God and the presence of God in your life now? If the experience of the presence of God you now recall was two years ago, does that mean your experience of God is not up-to-date? The psalmist speaks to that concern.

The second reason the psalmist could trust the Lord is that, not only had he seen God work in the past, but he was confident of God's purpose for God's people in the present. "But know that the Lord has set apart the godly for himself; the Lord hears when I call to him" (Psalm 4:3).

That's present tense. "The Lord *hears*." God gives us room when we are in distress. Relief and release may not come immediately, but they will come.

A friend of mine found God's release and help. Bill was one of God's unique persons. He fit no mold. He had an impish smile and a contagious sense of humor. He was scathingly honest, though loving and tender. He was one of my favorite people and was always a source of encouragement. He never presumed on my time, and I learned after a while that this was genuine care. If he called on the phone, he would usually begin, "Preacher, just thirty seconds," or "Preacher, give me one minute." And then he would give me his succinct, pungent, usually very helpful word.

He was always writing me notes. I would find them slipped under my study door or lying on the pulpit at the early worship service or taped to my kitchen door at home. They were put there early in the morning when most folks were still sleeping. His notes were as simple as "You knocked a home run yesterday, Preacher. Keep up the good work." Or, "Preacher, we need to praise God more—help us do that." Or, "I know you may be getting some criticism, but press on; the Lord is leading."

When Bill died, I went back and read some of his notes. One of them was a moving witness about facing problems and trusting God. I shared it at Bill's funeral.

Bill told of a long, dark period in which he felt trapped and abandoned. He talked about all his efforts to overcome the problem—including medicine, psychologists, tranquilizers—almost everything that we usually try. Then finally he faced up. This is what he wrote:

> I faced my problem in desperation, and in desperation I sought God. And God delivered me!
>
> Since he would not let me die, and I had asked Him to let me die, I promised Him, "God, you have a purpose for me. If you'll let me live a respectable life and free me from this bondage, every day you permit me to live, I'll serve you; and I'll never rob you again."
>
> Every day God stays at least ten paces ahead of me. I'm blessed every day in more ways than I can deserve, and nowhere can a happier man be found.

Bill had learned three lessons from the psalmist: One, face your problem; two, keep a prayer life going and growing; and three, trust the Lord.

Trust the Righteousness of God

In Psalm 11, there is an additional note to trusting God: Trust the *righteousness* of God. The psalmist is answering the question in verse 3, " 'If the foundations are destroyed, what can the righteous do'?" The answer is this:

> The Lord is in his holy temple,
>> the Lord's throne is in heaven;
>>> his eyes behold, his eyelids test, the children of men.
> The Lord tests the righteous and the wicked,
>> and his soul hates him that loves violence.
>>>>> (Psalm 11:4-5)

One of our failures as Christians is the little thought we give to the righteousness of God. That's the reason we lose perspective on life. That's the reason we give in to despair and become hopeless.

I think our problem is that we have misunderstood what righteousness is. We're not talking about a cold, hard list of things that are right and wrong. When the psalmist talks about God's righteousness, he's talking about God's commitment to do what is right in all situations. More than anything else, doing what is right means to do what a relationship requires. God's relationship to the wicked requires judgment; his relationship with the righteous requires blessing. David Allan Hubbard comments on Psalm 11:

> Just here our poet would want us to understand something else—what he means by the wicked and the righteous. These, too, are words of relationship. The wicked are those who care nothing about their relationship with God. The righteous are those for whom their covenant with God is the center of their living. Wickedness and righteousness are as much matters of commitment as of conduct, as much matters of attitude as of action, as much matters of devotion as of deeds.

As God scrutinizes men and women with those piercing, testing eyes, as he pointedly peers into the quality of our lives with eyelids lowered as though to help his focus, he is testing our loyalty more than our acts. Are we for him or against him? That is the essential question. Wicked people may do some good things, and righteous people may do some bad things. It is not sinfulness or sinlessness that is at stake. It is basic allegiance, ultimate loyalty.

The psalmist knew to whom he belonged; he was not at all ambivalent about his loyalty. That's why he could trust God's righteousness. He knew that God would do what his righteousness required—he would save the psalmist at the time and in the way he deemed best: "For the Lord is righteous, he loves righteous deeds" (v. 7). Our righteous deeds? Our acts of loyalty to God? Of course he loves them. But more important, he loves to do righteous deeds for us. Not our righteous deeds but God's righteous deeds are the theme of this song. God loves to deliver, to rescue, to save, to redeem those who look to him. That's an unbeatable assurance when we are tempted to drop out (Hubbard, pp. 36-37).

Trust the righteousness of God.

Count on the Power of God

There's yet another word the psalmist offers: Count on the power of God. Part of what the psalmist learned in the temple was the terrible judgment of God—that it would fall on those who did not pledge allegiance to the one true God. Their fate would recall the terrible destruction of Sodom and Gomorrah.

> On the wicked he will rain coals of fire and brimstone;
> a scorching wind shall be the portion of their cup.
>
> (Psalm 11:6)

I have an idea that the psalmist had heard that story of Sodom and Gomorrah often recounted in the temple. The rescue of Lot was an illustration of God's care for his own. The burning, searing devastation of Sodom and Gomorrah was an illustration of the terrors of judgment.

So, the psalmist could resist the tempting advice of his friends, "Flee like a bird to the mountains." He counted on the power of God. He had no need to flee.

How often have you been told in the midst of your trouble and difficulty to "hold on to God"? There is enough truth in that advice to make it worth our consideration. But, it misses the point if we have that idea as our understanding of what faith is about. Faith is not holding on to God; it's trusting God to hold on to *you,* even when you think you don't have a hold on God.

The issue with which we need to deal is that of our own willpower and God's power—God's grace. Barry Boulware, minister of Central United Methodist Church in Kansas City, Missouri, has told a story that vividly makes this distinction. It's the story of a highly successful businessman in a church where Boulware had served. This man's story was not an easy one. He had not been given the big breaks along his pathway to success. He had not inherited anything.

> He worked for everything he had, and over the years this hard work, combined with willpower, eventually paid off for him. I remember sitting in his office thinking that this guy could probably accomplish anything he would set his mind to do. And then he shattered my strong-man perception of him.
>
> He told me about the drinking problem he had suffered for several years. He had tried to keep it a secret from everyone, but eventually he had to face the fact that it was a disease and that he needed treatment. He entered an alcohol treatment center and was determined to beat his problem. Normally, a person is in treatment for about thirty days and is ready to be released. But not this man! After twenty-seven days, he had not experienced any real growth and decided he would discharge himself from the program.
>
> The next morning, on the twenty-eighth day of treatment, something happened to this man that has really changed his life and his perception of himself. Here is his story.
>
> "I had thought all along that these people were here to help me use my willpower. But finally I realized it had noth-

ing to do with willpower. Willpower is not the proper tool to use in trying to overcome something you cannot control. There was nothing I could will, there was nothing within my being that could affect the situation.

"Suddenly, I realized that the only help I could count on was grace . . . grace: a strength, a power, a force that was outside of me and other than me. For twenty-seven days I had tried to beat my disease by using sheer willpower. All through my life, willpower had always worked. But not this time. For it was only when I humbled myself, fell on my knees, admitted my total and unbroken, unconditional powerlessness—only then was I on my road to recovery."

Here was a man who knew grace and was known by grace. Here was a man who knew that strength and drive and willpower were not enough. Having heard his story, I asked him how he determines whether grace is needed or willpower is needed in certain situations he now confronts in his daily life. He said, "Each one of us is given a box containing two tools. Let's say one tool is a hammer and the other tool is a drill. If we need to drill a hole, the hammer won't be of any use. Try as we might, we cannot drill a hole with a hammer.

"Now let's say that we have another box. There are again two tools; one is willpower and the other is grace. Sometimes I need to use both of them. Other times I only need my own willpower. Sometimes, only grace is what will work."

It was then I asked him how he knew which tool to use. He didn't bat an eye; he didn't even flinch. He just looked at me with an air of spiritual confidence and quoted a well-known prayer used by twelve-step support groups:

"God grant me the Serenity to accept the things I cannot change, Courage to change the things I can, and Wisdom to know the difference" (Boulware, February 16, 1986).

The witness paints the picture clearly. We can't simply function by our own willpower. Of course there is a lot that we can do, a lot that our natural power can accomplish, but there comes a time when our strength alone is not sufficient. At that point we can be certain that we can count on God's power.

Rejoice in the Fellowship of God

The final advice of the psalmist for us when we want to run away is this: Rejoice in the fellowship of God. It is also good counsel for us when we feel trapped. It is excellent guidance for all conditions of life.

What a marvelous closing line the psalmist pens: "The upright shall behold his face" (11:7). Isn't this the psalmist's best word? What really keeps us from dropping out when the pressures mount? The joy of fellowship with God—being able to behold God's face.

More than any other part of the anatomy, the face expresses the person. To behold the face of God is to be in direct touch with God's magnificent love; it is to be personally acquainted with God's majestic holiness; it is to know firsthand God's unqualified acceptance.

In *Audacity to Believe,* Sheila Cassidy tells the moving story of her experience in Chile when she was arrested by Chile's Gestapo-style secret police after treating a wounded revolutionary. She was in solitary confinement for three weeks, and then for five weeks she was in a crowded detention camp with over one hundred female political prisoners. She eventually was found guilty of only a minor infringement of Chilean law at a trial shortly after her arrest, yet she was held without charges for fifty-nine days and then expelled from the country. She tells of an experience she had when she was kept for a period of time in a halfway house in solitary confinement. A doctor, for some unexplainable reason, brought her a Bible. It was half of a New Testament in a popular paperback edition, containing St. John's Gospel, the Acts of the Apostles, and the Letters of St. Paul. It was illustrated with charming line drawings.

Leafing idly through those portions of scripture and looking at the pictures, Sheila came across a drawing to illustrate the famous passage of Paul's Letter to the Romans:

Who, then, can separate us from the love of Christ? Can trouble do it, or hardship or persecution or hunger or poverty or danger or death? As the scripture says,

"For your sake we are in danger of death at all times;
we are treated like sheep that are going to be slaugh-
tered.".
No, in all these things we have complete victory through him
who loved us!

(Romans 8:35-37, TEV)

Sheila Cassidy reported:

When I looked at the drawing I knew what he meant, for
there was a man, naked and on his knees, buffeted by wind,
shielding his head from hurled stones and flying arrows.
Shooting across the page were the jagged lines which are
often used to represent lightning, but for me they were the
electricity, and there, stretched down to him, was the hand of
God.

... and yet
He was there.
I could only
close my eyes
and hold his hand
and grit my teeth
and know
with that cold, dark, naked knowing
that He was there.

Incredibly, in the midst of fear and loneliness I was filled
with joy, for I knew without any vestige of doubt that God was
with me, and that nothing that they could do to me could
change that (Cassidy, pp. 222-223).

Sheila Cassidy had experienced what the psalmist talked about:
rejoicing in the fellowship of God.

Flee to the mountains? Run away from it all? Drop out? Not at
all. Believe in the presence of God; trust in the righteousness of
God; count on the power of God; rejoice in the fellowship of God.

Our awareness and love of God, and especially God's awareness
and love of us, are more than enough to keep us from running
away, more than enough to release us when we feel trapped.

PSALM 27

The LORD is my light and my salvation;
   whom shall I fear?
The LORD is the stronghold of my life;
   of whom shall I be afraid?

When evildoers assail me,
   uttering slanders against me,
my adversaries and foes,
   they shall stumble and fall.

Though a host encamp against me,
   my heart shall not fear;
though war arise against me,
   yet I will be confident.

One thing have I asked of the LORD,
   that will I seek after;
that I may dwell in the house of the LORD
   all the days of my life,
to behold the beauty of the LORD
   and to inquire in his temple.

For he will hide me in his shelter
   in the day of trouble;
he will conceal me under the cover of his tent,

he will set me high upon a rock.
And now my head shall be lifted up
   above my enemies round about me;
and I will offer in his tent
   sacrifices with shouts of joy;
I will sing and make melody to the LORD.

Hear, O LORD, when I cry aloud,
   be gracious to me and answer me!
Thou hast said, "Seek ye my face."
   My heart says to thee,
"Thy face, LORD, do I seek."
   Hide not thy face from me.

Turn not thy servant away in anger,
   thou who hast been my help.
Cast me not off, forsake me not,
   O God of my salvation!
For my father and my mother have forsaken me,
   but the LORD will take me up.

Teach me thy way, O LORD;
   and lead me on a level path
   because of my enemies.
Give me not up to the will of my adversaries;
   for false witnesses have risen against me,
   and they breathe out violence.

I believe that I shall see the goodness of the LORD
   in the land of the living!
Wait for the LORD;
   be strong, and let your heart take courage;
   yea, wait for the LORD!

PSALM 10

Why dost thou stand afar off, O LORD?
    Why dost thou hide thyself in times of trouble?
In arrogance the wicked hotly pursue the poor;
    let them be caught in the schemes which they have devised.
For the wicked boasts of the desires of his heart,
    and the man greedy for gain curses and renounces the LORD.
In the pride of his countenance the wicked does not seek him;
    all his thoughts are, "There is no God."

His ways prosper at all times;
    thy judgments are on high, out of his sight;
    as for all his foes, he puffs at them.
He thinks in his heart, "I shall not be moved;
    throughout all generations I shall not meet adversity."

His mouth is filled with cursing and deceit and oppression;
    under his tongue are mischief and iniquity.
He sits in ambush in the villages;
    in hiding places he murders the innocent.

His eyes stealthily watch for the hapless,
    he lurks in secret like a lion in his covert;
he lurks that he may seize the poor,
    he seizes the poor when he draws him into his net.

The hapless is crushed, sinks down,
    and falls by his might.
He thinks in his heart, "God has forgotten,
    he has hidden his face, he will never see it."

Arise, O LORD; O God, lift up thy hand;
    forget not the afflicted.
Why does the wicked renounce God,
    and say in his heart, "Thou wilt not call to account"?

Thou dost see; yea, thou dost note trouble and vexation,
 that thou mayst take it into thy hands;
the hapless commits himself to thee;
 thou hast been the helper of the fatherless.

Break thou the arm of the wicked and evildoer;
 seek out his wickedness till thou find none.
The LORD is king for ever and ever;
 the nations shall perish from his land.

O LORD, thou wilt hear the desire of the meek;
 thou wilt strengthen their heart, thou wilt incline thy ear
to do justice to the fatherless and the oppressed,
 so that man who is of the earth may strike terror no more.

THREE

A CONFIDENCE FOR ALL SEASONS

*I*n London a few years ago I saw Robert Bolt's play, *A Man for All Seasons.* It's a moving, illuminating, challenging, dramatic presentation on the life of Sir Thomas More. There's a note of judgment in it, a strong note that makes us wonder, and even anguish, about the depth of our commitments.

In the closing scene of the play, things are intense. Cromwell is having his way, the court is fixed, and there is no escape for Sir Thomas More. He will not violate his conscience, and he will not compromise his integrity by playing the petty political game.

The man whose false witness condemns him is a man More had befriended. Richard, now Sir Richard, has been a conniving, scheming, cunning, step-on-and-over-anyone person to get position and power. When Richard lies in his death-dealing witness, More shows grace and humor—two of the characteristics that make him "the man for all seasons." He asks Richard about the medallion, the Red Dragon, which Richard is displaying proudly around his neck.

Cromwell answers for Richard: "Sir Richard is appointed Attorney-General for Wales."

Looking into Richard's face with pain and amusement, More says, "For Wales? Why, Richard, it profits a man nothing to give his soul for the whole world . . . but for Wales?"

It was a word of humor—and of stinging judgment. Sir Thomas More, "a man for all seasons," had a confidence for all seasons, and he kept his head higher than his enemies.

PSALM 27: I WILL BE CONFIDENT

That's what we need—confidence when we face all of our enemies. That's what Psalm 27 is about. It's about shelter and protection. There are two words in it that resonate in all of us: *fear* and *confidence*. Both words are in that almost unbelievable testimony we find in verse 3: "Though a host encamp against me, my heart shall not fear; though war rise against me, yet I will be confident."

That's the reason I have titled this book and this chapter "A Confidence for All Seasons." Isn't that our need? And isn't that what God provides for us—confidence in the midst of fear and trouble?

It's confidence that enables us "to keep our heads above our enemies." That image in verse 6 strikes a responsive chord: "And now my head shall be lifted up above my enemies round about me."

I'm not talking about "people" enemies alone. I'm talking about negative emotions, trials, temptations, sorrow, and trouble. As the psalmist says in verse 5: God "will conceal me under the cover of his tent, he will set me high upon a rock."

Maybe we should begin by thinking about the "hosts," mentioned in verse 3, that encamp about us, causing us to fear. Is there a more common enemy to all of us than fear itself? Is any enemy more devastating?

One of my all-time favorite "Peanuts" comic strips by cartoonist Charles Schultz locates Charlie Brown in the school nurse's office. As he waits, he observes: "So here I am about to see the school nurse."

Then Charlie wonders: "She'll probably take my temperature and look at my throat. . . ." Then he worries: "Maybe she'll take a blood sample. I hope she doesn't take a blood sample. Maybe she'll just weigh me."

And finally, Charlie agonizes, "If she mentions exploratory surgery, I'll scream!"

I'm a lot like Charlie Brown. Most of us are, aren't we? We often let our fears run away with us. We live in an anxious age, and we've grown accustomed to borrowing trouble. It's a trait of our lives. We live *on edge* more often than we live in peace and confidence.

We fear economic setback and loss. Reflect upon the conversations you've had this past week. I would be surprised if you did not have some occasion to express or hear someone else express fear about the economic situation.

We fear the future. This is a sort of floating fear that we can't always name or specify. Many times it's vague, but it stirs within, leaving us unsettled and uncertain. It has to do with the core issue of being human and thus being vulnerable to hazards, some of which threaten our physical being and that of those we love.

So we fear the future because change is such a distinctive characteristic of our daily lives. Nothing seems permanent anymore. There are no stakes of certainty driven down in the human venture. One writer expresses it:

> When I was young and my world was dominated by inde-
> structible adults, I learned an ancient way of thinking that is
> as dangerous as a rotten step on a ladder. It told me that some
> things would remain unchanged: My grandfather who meant
> so much to me; the trail through our wood lot into the timber
> beyond; the feeling of the lake on a hot summer day's swim;
> the colors when I open my new pencil box on the first day of
> school. . . . But my grandfather died; a developer bulldozed
> the woodlot; lumberjacks cut down the timbers; the lake is
> polluted and posted against swimming, and pencil boxes are
> not what they used to be (Shelby, May 19, 1985).

We could go on and on. We fear death, we fear abandonment, we fear losing a loved one either by death or divorce. We fear being cut off, ostracized. We fear the loss of friends and the loss of whatever social status we have.

In other words, the hosts of fear encamp about us.

Manageable Troubles

Given the fact of fear, let's think about how confidence in God's love and care can be our stronghold for living even in the midst of trouble. First, begin at a low rung on the ladder: Some of our troubles are quite manageable. They devastate us because we *fear* them. Within themselves they have no destructive power. It is our fear that invests them with power. Pay attention to that because it is a key for living, as the psalmist said, above the heads of our enemies.

You have heard of the woman who said, "I don't believe in ghosts, but I'm afraid of them." We're afraid of so many things which, in themselves, have no power to hurt us, except through the torment of the fears they inspire. Wallace Hamilton reminds us that

> The dread of illness can be more damaging than the illness. The fear of failure can be more fatal than the failure. Go through the list of phobias which have multiplied in an age of anxiety and see how many of them are what Archibald MacLeish called "faceless fears." That is, they have no substance, no shape, no bodily image that you can face or fight. They're shadows. Fear of the dark—fear of open places—fear of closed places—fear of criticism—fear of the future—fear of old age—fear of death—all the way to phobophobia, which is fear of fear. There are seventy-two listed phobias, most of them shadows, ghosts. They have no power to hurt except through fear of them.
>
> Obviously then, one of the great needs of life is to keep our fears manageable. And one of the great contributions that religious faith makes to wholesome life is right here. Nothing takes the fear out of life so much as an awareness deep within of God's nearness and His loving concern. "I will fear no evil for thou art with me." The particular dread the psalmist speaks about is the common fear of death. He likens it to a shadow: "though I walk through the valley of the shadow of death. . . ." There's nothing much to fear in a shadow. The shadow of a dog can't bite. The shadow of a snake can't sting. And when life is undergirded by a consciousness of God's presence and concern, we're released from the fear of many

shadows and get beyond the reach of many seeming evils (Hamilton, pp. 50-51).

We need to see how manageable our troubles would be if we did not allow our fears to debilitate us to the point that we can't deal with them. We need to see how manageable they would be if we allowed ourselves to trust God.

Curses Become Blessings

A second rung on the ladder is this: Some of our troubles, some evils that have happened to us, can be turned into something positive, rather than negative. Our troubles and problems can be a blessing rather than a curse. They can provide power, rather than make us powerless victims.

We can get beyond the reach of the power of our troubles to hurt us when we confront them, not with resentment but with resourcefulness. We can learn to use our trouble to add new dimensions to our lives.

Much as we hate trouble, complain about it, and try to avoid it if we can, as we look back over our lives we can be grateful for those very things which, when they happened, seemed hostile. We know in retrospect that their challenge was the cause for growth, and some of the things which we hated when they happened were really channels of grace.

Think about your own life. What is it that has given your character substance? What is it that has endowed you with strength? What is it that sets you apart as a unique person? What is it that has sharpened your natural endowments and made them serve you well? What is it that has equipped you in faith and commitment and brought you to a place of trustful reliance on God?

When we answer these questions, we will discover the roles that trouble and misfortune have played in our life.

Wendell Wilkie said, "What a man needs to get ahead is a powerful enemy." Edmund Burke said, "Our antagonist is our helper. He that wrestles with us strengthens our muscles and sharpens our skill." Apparently human nature must have something to push against and something to wrestle with. I suppose this is the hopeful thing about handicaps. . . . Handicaps are the hard things we wrestle with and push against.

Dr. Marie Ray, a psychiatrist of some note, after making a wide study of the relation between handicaps and achievements, and going down the list of notable men and women, came up with this conclusion, that most of the shining lights of history were made so by their struggles with either some disability or some responsibility that seemed too great for their powers. And then she put down this definite rule as the result of her research. "No one succeeds without a handicap. No one succeeds in spite of a handicap. When anyone succeeds, it is because of a handicap" (Hamilton, pp. 51-52).

We don't want to minimize in the least the tragic elements of life. We don't want to glamorize the trouble and the heartache and the difficulty. We don't want to disregard or make light of the heavy load that so many people carry. Still, we recognize this fact: More often than not, our troubles and problems and burdens can be a blessing rather than a curse. They can provide power, rather than turn us into powerless victims.

Divine Protection

Now the third rung on the ladder gets us into another area of concern that Psalm 27 suggests: the whole area of divine protection. There is ultimate protection from all our enemies, divine protection for those who trust in the Lord. This gives us a confidence for all seasons.

Many of you still remember the story that took place back in 1984 in Mason, Tennessee. Louise DeGrafinried astounded the nation when she persuaded an escaped convict from a Tennessee prison to surrender. He came brandishing a gun, and with the gun he thought he was in control. He had surprised Nathan, Louise's husband, outside their modest home and forced him inside at gunpoint. Amazingly, she was not afraid of the gun. This short, grandmotherly woman told the prisoner to put down the gun while she fixed him some breakfast. Surprisingly, the prisoner did it. Then, this mild-mannered woman spoke to this young man about her faith in Jesus Christ and about how he could have a better life if he accepted Christ. When the breakfast was prepared, they said grace together around the table, and Louise prayed for that young man. They ate breakfast together, and then a shocking thing happened; the young escapee telephoned the authorities. Before long he was on his way back to the Tennessee prison.

Note the different focus of power and security. The young man thought his power and his security were in that gun. With that gun, he thought he was in control. But Louise trusted an ultimate authority, and by trusting in that authority she overcame her fears. She had a confidence for all seasons. With the power of her commitment and the security of her love and trust in God, perhaps for the first time in his life, that desperate and confused young man was offered peace with Jesus Christ.

It's very easy to confuse meaning when we talk about protection. I hear, almost weekly, someone talking too glibly about it. The way some people talk about protection, you would think God wouldn't even allow them to stump their toes—much less allow a disease or an accident to invade their family circle.

It's almost obscene to talk about divine protection in that fashion. In fact, it is obscene—especially when you put such glib utterances up against the pain and suffering of many Christians in the world today. When I think of all the people who have died for the faith, and for causes such as human freedom and justice, even during the past fifty years, I don't think glibly about protection.

Even in our daily conversation we need to be careful about glibness. "The Lord saved me from that terror," someone said, when just yesterday, the word came that a friend's wife, forty-five years old, had died of cancer.

When we talk about divine protection, we're talking about something ultimate. When we talk about it, we ought to do so in a low voice of reticence and humility, not in the certainty that smacks of arrogance and suggests spiritual pride, that takes no note of people as faithful as we are who have not been protected in the way we use the word. Divine protection doesn't keep us from being crucified. It didn't keep Jesus from the cross.

Look at the movement of Psalm 27 in the last few verses:

Teach me thy way, O Lord;
   and lead me on a level path. . . .
Give me not up to the will of my adversaries;
for false witnesses . . . breathe out violence.
(Psalm 27:11-12)

You see he has not been delivered from trouble—but he knows an ultimate protection. His enemies may destroy his body, but not his soul. Listen to the last confident but humble breathings of his prayer:

I believe that I shall see the goodness of the Lord
   in the land of the living!
Wait for the Lord;
   be strong, and let your heart take courage.
(Psalm 27:13-14)

That's confidence—confidence for all seasons.

The psalms are full of this expression of trust which makes us confident of protection. The classic and best-known is the Twenty-Third Psalm, at which we will look in chapter seven. We all remember that bold affirmation, "I will fear no evil; for thou art with me."

What do these verses mean? They mean what they say. The Lord will protect us and save us in the way that matters—ultimately. God may not protect us from trouble by shielding us from it—but God will protect us *in* trouble. God may not save us *from* death, but God will save us *in* death.

In reflecting on Psalm 27, we have suggested three lessons. One, many of our problems and troubles are manageable. They have no destructive power except as we allow our fear to give them power.

Two, some of our troubles, even the evil that comes to us, can be converted from enemies to friends; so our problems and troubles can be blessings, not curses.

Three, there is ultimate protection from all our enemies—divine protection for those who trust the Lord.

Let's turn now to Psalm 10 for confidence when God seems far off.

PSALM 10: WHY DOST THOU STAND AFAR OFF?

I remember the story of the California realtor who once persuaded Groucho Marx to inspect a palatial oceanfront estate that was for sale. The salesman drove the comedian up the mile-long road leading into the estate. Then he escorted Groucho through the house, stables, gardens, and kennels, demonstrating the many beautiful features of the dream palace by the sea. Groucho patiently plodded after him, nodding from time to time, apparently somewhat impressed. Finally he was ushered out onto the flagstone terrace, and the salesman waved proudly toward the broad expanse of the Pacific. "Now what do you think?" he asked the comedian. "I don't care for it," replied Groucho thoughtfully, as he pointed toward the gorgeous view. "Take away the ocean, and then what have you got?"

Groucho was being his funny self. The truth is, you can't take away the ocean. And a larger truth is you can't take away the confidence when we cultivate the faith and trust of the psalmist: "Though a host encamp against me, my heart shall not fear."

It's a confidence for all seasons!

But it's not all that easy to live in confidence, is it? Even though we strive for it, there are those times in our lives when we are adrift, frightened, uncertain of the future, without the strength it seems we need to take the next step of faith. We want to cry out with the psalmist: "Why dost thou stand afar off, O Lord? Why dost thou hide thyself in times of trouble?" (Psalm 10:1).

I identify with the psalmist. There have been times in my life when God seemed far off, beyond the reach of communication. I have awakened at three o'clock in the morning, morning after morning after morning, feeling anguished in spirit until daybreak; but my praying was more frustrating than fruitful. My passionate pleas seemed to bounce off the ceiling and ricochet around the walls.

It never shocks me when a person comes to my office and is hardly settled in his chair before he or she blurts out: "Preacher, I can't pray; there's no connection—I feel no presence. God has left me."

Anyone who reads the Bible shouldn't be shocked to hear that kind of confession from another or to feel it in his or her own soul. The Bible, which serves us well as an entree to God and as a channel to bring us closer to God, shares honestly persons' feelings of God's being far off, absent, silent, and beyond their reach.

The unknown writer of Psalm 10 expressed these feelings in words that resonate the pain of a heart groping for God but unable to make contact. These are anguishing questions that boil up from the depths of a despairing soul: "Why dost thou stand afar off, O Lord? Why dost thou hide thyself in times of trouble?" (Psalm 10:1).

> To the tearful eye of the sufferer, the Lord seemed to *stand* still, as if he calmly looked on, and did not sympathize with his afflicted one. Nay, more, the Lord appeared to be *afar off*, no longer "a very present help in trouble," but an inaccessible mountain into which no man would be able to climb. The presence of God is the joy of his people, but any suspicion of his absence is distracting beyond measure" (Spurgeon, p. 123).

"Why dost thou hide thyself in times of trouble?" Spurgeon rightly reminds us that "it is not the trouble, but the hiding of our Father's face, which cuts us to the quick."

Telling God How We Feel

I sat with a woman recently who felt God's face was hidden from her. "I've failed God," she anguished. Her marriage had ended in a nasty divorce, and she was not only taking the burden upon herself, she was feeling no hint of the presence of God. She needed to tell God just how she felt.

In Psalm 10, the writer minces no words in telling God how he feels. We're not to be silent sufferers. Even though God seems far off, even though a large question mark is superimposed over our prayer, still we tell God how we feel.

God's absence is almost never felt when things are going well. When the seas are smooth, the sky is bright, we just assume that God is on hand, taking care of us. But let the tension build and the frustrations mount, let life put its knee in our stomach and start to pin us to the mat, and we begin to wonder, where is God?

When this happens, do what the psalmist did. Tell God how you feel. Doing so will remind you that God is near enough to hear your complaints.

There is a television ad that pictures a woman trying to get a particular brand of food in a grocery store. When it is not available, she becomes irate with the clerk, demanding to know why she can't have it. The poor clerk calls the frantic manager, who calls someone in a distant warehouse, who calls a distributor, who calls a posh skyscraper office somewhere in "the great beyond." But no one answers the phone. God's program is not like that.

Though God may not be doing all that the psalmist wants *when* he wants it, God is within reach of the psalmist's prayer. The psalmist knows this and raises his complaint to God.

He doesn't spare the details. What he feels, he says. Thoroughly and forcefully, he describes his problem in all its ramifications. In verse after verse the psalmist reminds God of what his enemies are doing. Then earnestly, passionately, he calls on God to act: "Arise, O Lord; O God, lift up thy hand; forget not the afflicted" (Psalm 10:12).

By telling God what he feels, he both unburdens his own spirit and expresses his trust in God. This is a key understanding. In sharing honestly with God how we feel, we both unburden our spirit and express our trust in God.

I've seen this happen so completely in corporate sharing and prayer. When a few people are together because they need each other and are seeking to grow in their Christian walk, release and relief comes when some person breaks through his or her reservations or fear of trusting feelings to others. For instance, to be able to say to another, "I'm afraid," is a relief valve with saving potential. The fear may have many causes:

"I'm afraid I'm going to die."

"I'm afraid my wife will never get well."

"I'm afraid that I'll take that drink or smoke that joint or pop that pill that will send me careening back into the darkness and helplessness of drug dependency."

"I'm afraid it has gone on too long—my indifference, my calloused unconcern, my putting money and job and success above my family. I'm afraid it's too late, that I've lost my wife's and children's love. I'm afraid."

Fear is only one feeling. To be able to tell others about those feelings of fear, or any other deep or tumultuous feelings that are about to explode within us, unburdens our spirit. It is dangerous to our physical health, as well as to our emotional and spiritual health, to keep those feelings bottled up inside. Sooner or later, they will break out—maybe as ulcers, stress that brings a heart attack, anxiety that brings a nervous collapse, rage that does harm to someone we love, or as a loss of faith that undermines the possibility of spiritual healing.

In my counseling with persons about to be married, I always offer two bits of advice. One, don't expect your mate to know what you are thinking and feeling without your verbalizing it. Two, "do not let the sun go down on your anger." Both have to do with sharing our feelings.

Interestingly, sharing our feelings with others is often the dynamic that will enable us to share those feelings with God. When we do that, we're back at the needed place for further release and relief; we're back at the point of trusting God. That's a primary insistence of the psalmist: Share honestly with God how you feel.

Trusting God's Judgment

The confidence we need—a confidence for all seasons—is restored when we know that God's judgment is certain. When God seems far off, we tend to forget that!

The psalmist asks, "Why does the wicked renounce God, and say in his heart, 'Thou wilt not call to account'?" (Psalm 10:13). Before the question he has described the harsh deeds and bitter attitudes of the wicked:

> In arrogance the wicked hotly pursue the poor;
>> let them be caught in the schemes which they have
>> devised.

For the wicked boasts of the desires of his heart,
    and the man greedy for gain curses and renounces the
    Lord.
In the pride of his countenance the wicked does not seek
    him;
    all his thoughts are, "There is no God."

(Psalm 10:2-4)

He piles up the evidence, as though he needs to convince God to judge, and to judge righteously. Both the psalmist and the wicked seem to think that God's silence is a sign of unconcern, of uninvolvement. God is removed, so the wicked think, remote from their evil ways. So, for both the righteous and the wicked, God seems far off. The wicked go ever further in thought and action. "In the pride of his countenance the wicked does not seek him; all his thoughts are, 'There is no God' " (Psalm 10:4).

The psalmist makes his assessment of the situation of the wicked:

His ways prosper at all times;
    thy judgments are on high, out of his sight;
    as for all his foes, he puffs at them.
He thinks in his heart, "I shall not be moved;
    throughout all generations I shall not meet adversity."

(Psalm 10:5-6)

In that assessment is a penetrating truth: "Thy judgments are on high, out of his sight." God's judgments are not always seen. They don't fit into our time frame, and often they are veiled from our discernment. The mills of God grind slowly, but they do grind. God may not settle debts every month—but God's debts will be settled. One day, probably in this life—but if not in this life, then in a final reckoning beyond death—every person will account for his or her deeds. The psalmist is warning us not to make the same mistake as the wicked.

One of the loyal and effective witnesses for Jesus in the social upheavals of these recent decades was A. J. Muste. A reporter once asked this gentle, but committed, protagonist for Jesus why he wasted his time in lonely vigils and obscure places for the

67

cause of peace and in the struggle for human dignity for all people. The reporter asked what good Muste thought was being accomplished when war still raged and people were denied their rights. Muste answered that he did what he did, not to change the world, but to keep the world from changing him.

We must fight against the mistaken notion of the wicked, who think that God "will not call into account." Indeed, God will.

Being Strengthened in Our Faith

Knowing this—that God's judgment is certain—we can be strengthened in our faith even when God seems far off. The psalmist finds it so; and before he finishes the psalm, his confidence is restored.

> The Lord is king for ever and ever;
>   the nations shall perish from his land.
>
> O Lord, thou wilt hear the desire of the meek;
>   thou wilt strengthen their heart,
>   thou wilt incline thy ear
> to do justice to the fatherless and the oppressed,
>   so that man who is of the earth may strike
>   terror no more.
>   (Psalm 10:16-18)

Don't forget that this word is set against the complaint that the poor and oppressed, the widowed and orphaned were being used and exploited by sinful people, and God seemed nowhere about. Deep down the psalmist knew better. Despite the fact that God seemed silent and removed, the psalmist knew that God's love and care was constant, that God's character was changeless. Sooner or later God would speak and act. You and I can count on that, too. Read the encouraging words of the hymn "Once to Every Man and Nation":

> Though the cause of evil prosper,
> Yet 'tis truth alone is strong;
> Though her portion be the scaffold,

And upon the throne be wrong:
Yet that scaffold sways the future,
And, behind the dim unknown,
Standeth God within the shadow
Keeping watch above his own.

Not only in the social arena, but in our personal lives as well, we can be strengthened by the experience of feeling God's absence, becoming certain of God's ultimate presence. Martin Luther King, Jr. witnesses to this in his book *Strength to Love:*

> On a particular Monday evening, following a tension-packed week which included being arrested and receiving numerous threatening telephone calls, I spoke at a mass meeting. I attempted to convey an overt impression of strength and courage, although I was inwardly depressed and fear-stricken. At the end of the meeting, Mother Pollard came to the front of the church and said, "Come here, son." I immediately went to her and hugged her affectionately. "Something is wrong with you," she said. "You didn't talk strong tonight." Seeking further to disguise my fears, I retorted, "Oh, no, Mother Pollard, nothing is wrong. I am feeling as fine as ever." But her insight was discerning. "Now you can't fool me," she said. "I knows something is wrong. Is it that we ain't doing things to please you? Or is it that the white folks is bothering you?" Before I could respond, she looked directly into my eyes and said, "I done told you we is with you all the way." Then her face became radiant and she said in words of quiet certainty, "But even if we ain't with you, God's gonna take care of you." As she spoke those consoling words, everything in me quivered and quickened with the pulsing tremor of raw energy.
>
> Since that dreary night in 1956, Mother Pollard has passed on to glory and I have known very few quiet days. I have been tortured without and tormented within by the raging fires of tribulation. I have been forced to muster what strength and courage I have to withstand howling winds of pain and jostling storms of adversity. But as the years have unfolded the eloquently simple words of Mother Pollard have come back again and again to give light and peace and guidance to

my troubled soul. "God's gonna take care of you" (King, p. 117).

So God does!

So God will!

Even when God seems far off, we can know the restoration of confidence if we will share honestly with God how we feel; if we will trust the fact that God's judgment is sure; and if we will be strengthened in faith by what we are experiencing—even though we feel like God is absent.

PSALM 56

Be gracious to me, O God, for men trample upon me;
   all day long foemen oppress me;
my enemies trample upon me all day long,
   for many fight against me proudly.
When I am afraid,
   I put my trust in thee.
In God, whose word I praise,
   in God I trust without a fear.
   What can flesh do to me?

All day long they seek to injure my cause;
   all their thoughts are against me for evil.
They band themselves together, they lurk,
   they watch my steps.
As they have waited for my life,
   so recompense them for their crime;
   in wrath cast down the peoples, O God!

Thou hast kept count of my tossings;
   put thou my tears in thy bottle!
   Are they not in thy book?
Then my enemies will be turned back
   in the day when I call.
   This I know, that God is for me.

In God, whose word I praise,
   in the LORD, whose word I praise,
in God I trust without a fear.
   What can man do to me?
My vows to thee I must perform, O God;
   I will render thank offerings to thee.
For thou hast delivered my soul from death,
   yea, my feet from falling,
that I may walk before God
   in the light of life.

FOUR

PUT THOU MY TEARS
IN THY BOTTLE

*T*here are a lot of images in the Psalms—powerful, descriptive, suggestive images.

"My Lord is my rock, and my fortress" (Psalm 18:2).

The Lord "will conceal me under the cover of his tent" (Psalm 27:5*b*).

"The Lord sits enthroned as king for ever" (29:10*b*).

The images abound. God is seen as a safe harbor and as the safe arms of a shepherd. Our life is graphically described: We pass through the valley of the shadow of death, we walk by still waters, and we rest in green pastures.

How rich, how very rich are the expressions of emotion in the description of the experiences of the psalmist.

How beseeching is Psalm 39, verse 12: "Hear my prayer, O Lord, and give ear to my cry; hold not thy peace at my tears! For I am thy passing guest, a sojourner, like all my fathers."

How honest is Psalm 6, verse 7: "My eye wastes away because of grief, it grows weak because of all my foes."

And how graphic is Psalm 124, verse 7: "We have escaped as a bird from the snare of the fowlers; the snare is broken, and we have escaped!"

And how beautiful the confidence of Psalm 131, verse 2: "But I have calmed and quieted my soul, like a child quieted at its mother's breast."

PSALM 56: PUT THOU
MY TEARS IN THY BOTTLE

There is one image in Psalm 56 that may at first strike a quizzical rather than a familiar note in your mind. It's the image I'm using as the title of this chapter: "Put thou my tears in thy bottle." It's a part of verse 8 of Psalm 56: "Thou hast kept count of my tossings; put thou my tears in thy bottle! Are they not in thy book?"

In this particular psalm, it's not the "tears" of the psalmist that is new. The psalmist is always talking about tears. But it's the image connected with the tears in this particular petition that grabs my attention: "Put thou my tears in thy bottle."

In her book, *Strange Scriptures That Perplex the Western Mind* (Eerdmans, 1940), Barbara M. Bowen provides some background on the image the psalmist may have been referring to. She describes the old custom of collecting the tears of a family and preserving the tears in bottles. When death or serious trouble occurred, each member of the family brought his or her tear bottle and collected tears from all the persons present. These bottles were sacred to the family members because they represented all the sorrows of the family. Each person was buried with his or her tear bottle. Many of these have been found in ancient tombs.

I had an experience recently that enriched this image of the psalmist for me. I was counseling with a young woman, Leigh Hobson, who had recently lost one of the most important persons in her life—a great-aunt who was almost a mother to her. It was painful—and she had done a lot of crying, which is cleansing and healing.

One morning, Leigh's six-year-old daughter, Katy, witnessing her mother's grief, painted her a picture and gave it, with some other love tokens, to her mom and said, "I want you to feel better."

That night when Leigh was tucking Katy into bed she thanked her and told her that her love gifts did make her feel better. Then she added, "But Katy, I want you to know that Mommy may cry a lot more, because I loved Ola so much."

"But Mommy," Katy said, "I'm afraid you'll turn into a tear."

"Well," said Leigh, "If I turned into a tear, would you wipe me up?"

"No," said Katy, "I'd put you into my eye."

Wow! What perception and wisdom—what a picture of love! The psalmist was praying that somehow God would take his tears, use them, make them God's own—and, yes, even redeem them.

I'm indebted to my friend Dow Kirkpatrick for bringing two historically separated verses of scripture together in a meaningful way. There is no affinity between the verses from the books of Jeremiah and Second Corinthians, yet they provide a real commentary on what we do with pain and suffering. The Moffatt translation of Jeremiah 51:58 is, "Pagans waste their pains." Paul, centuries later, speaks of pains that are not wasted: "The pain God is allowed to guide ends in a saving repentance never to be regretted" (2 Cor. 7:10, Moffatt). Growth is dependent upon whether we *waste* or *guide* our suffering (Kirkpatrick, January 28, 1968).

Suffering is a part of life. The psalmist knew this. We may get by without suffering for a season, but not forever. Some of us know far more suffering than others, and this we don't understand. What we do with our suffering is the crucial question. The decisive factor in human life is not the conditions that surround us, but our response to them. We can "waste" our suffering by allowing it to embitter us, to make us hard and harsh, calloused and cynical. Or we can use it and guide it for our growth.

In a sharing group we were talking about the meaning of Jesus' words in the Sermon on the Mount, "No one can serve two masters. . . . You cannot serve God and mammon. . . . Do not be anxious about your life. . . . Seek first his kingdom" (Matt. 6:24, 25, 33).

I asked the question, "What would you do if suddenly you received a gift of a million dollars?" I was amazed at the honesty of the group. They actually admitted the priorities they currently held, and we were moved by the answer of one lady.

"I would give the greatest portion of it to the Heart Fund," she said.

We knew her story. Her thirty-five-year-old dentist husband had been stricken with a heart attack. He barely survived. Suddenly their well-planned world was shattered. The security they thought they had was sand beneath their feet. His busy dental practice couldn't be sustained. Their entire life was thrown into upheaval.

"We learned in this," the young woman said, "that life has other priorities than what we had set—that the real security is in our relationship to God, not to things. This catastrophe has completely reordered our lives."

Guiding suffering, rather than wasting it! For Christians this ought to be an obvious truth. We can learn about suffering, if we like, from the horrendous happenings of life. Or, we can learn it from the heart of our faith—from a God who suffered in Jesus Christ. We can see the cross as another sadistic mode of execution, or we can carry the outcome of Jesus' death and resurrection in our hearts and celebrate the new life we have because of it. We can look at the tortured pains of life and wonder about the capricious injustice of it. Or, we can look into the eyes of God, who suffered by choice, and discover the ennobling difference suffering can make if we guide it rather than waste it.

So the psalmist prays, "Put thou my tears in thy bottle." Long before the cross—the picture of a loving, suffering God—this person did not want his suffering to be wasted.

The psalmist was confident that God cared about his suffering. The psalmist affirms, "Thou hast kept count of my tossings." Isn't that a beautiful image? Think about it. In the midnight hours we toss and turn, our emotions fevered with fear, our minds contorting with confusion and frustration because nothing is working out. We face an ominous day tomorrow, and we don't know what we are going to do; we don't know where we are going to get the money to pay the bill, the strength to meet the challenge, the courage to face our difficulty. We toss and we turn. Wouldn't it be something if we would stay aware of the fact that the Lord keeps count of our tossings, that the Lord knows what's going on with us? The psalmist remembered this: "Thou has kept count of my tossings. Put thou my tears in thy bottle! Are they not in thy book?"

The psalmist was certain that God was taking note of him and knew what was going on in his life, in his tossings and turnings. But, more than that, the Lord knew the whole sweep of his life—his life span has been recorded in God's book. It's that conviction of the psalmist—the conviction that God knows and cares—that enables him to pray that remarkable prayer.

God Is for Me

There are some phrases in this prayer, mostly affirmations, that we may claim for strength and guidance.

First, the second part of verse 9: "This I know, that God is for me." What a person knows is very important. There's a classic story that I've heard a number of preachers tell that illustrates this:

> One day in London an atheist sought to make sport of an unlettered man who had been converted only a few years before. "Do you know anything about Jesus Christ?" he asked. "Yes, by the grace of God, I do," was the answer. "When was he born?" was the next question. But the ignorant saint gave an incorrect answer. "How old was he when he died?" Again, the answer was incorrect. Other questions were asked with the same result until the atheist said with a sneer, "See—you do not know as much about Jesus as you thought, do you?" "I know all too little," was his modest answer, "but I know this: Three years ago I was one of the worst drunkards in the East End of London. Three years ago my wife was a broken-hearted woman, and my children were as afraid of me as if I had been a wild beast. Today I have one of the happiest homes in London, and when I come home at the close of the day my wife and children are glad to see me. Jesus Christ has done this for me. This I know" (Chappell, pp. 94-95).

What a person knows is very important. "This I know," the psalmist said, "that God is for me." You can't beat that, can you? To know that God *is* is not enough. The psalmist is witnessing to a personal knowledge that goes beyond theory and speculation, beyond philosophy or theology. He has gone beyond evidences, rational speculation, and intellectual argument into a firsthand knowledge of God.

This I know, that God is for me. This may be our most important conviction. It is because of what the psalmist knows that he makes some of his other astounding affirmations.

Confidence in Calamity

Look at one of the affirmations in verse 3: "When I am afraid, I put my trust in thee." There are two facets of truth that call for our consideration here, two ways of looking at this affirmation.

The first is a question: Does it take calamity to turn us to God? We don't know precisely what situation the psalmist was talking about, but it must have been pretty bad. Note some phrases from the first verses of the psalm: "foemen oppress me"; "enemies trample upon me all day long"; "their thoughts are against me for evil"; "they lurk, they watch my steps" (Psalm 56:1, 2, 5, 6).

It was a calamitous time for the psalmist. Yet, I think it's safe to assume that the psalmist did not turn to the Lord only in time of calamity. There was that ongoing relationship that had cultivated his confidence.

I remember when Randy, to whom I have dedicated this book and of whom I wrote in the introduction, was smitten with cancer. To get that news was an emotionally shattering experience. Randy is forty-one years old, and he and his wife, Nancy, have two little children. He had just begun his business and was getting established on his own. Then came this devastating word—*cancer*. He had tumors in his lymphatic system, in the lining of the brain, and in the bone marrow.

Randy's response was inspiring. In the hospital for his treatment of fourth-stage lymphoma, he shared with my wife, Jerry, a word he had just read from *The Book of Common Prayer*. It was from the section on "Prayers for use by a Sick Person":

> This is another day, O Lord. I know not what it will bring forth, but make me ready, Lord, for whatever it may be. If I am to stand up, help me to stand bravely. If I am to sit still, help me to sit quietly. If I am to lie low, help me to do it patiently. And if I am to do nothing, let me do it gallantly. Make these words more than words, and give me the spirit of Jesus. Amen (1979 Edition, p. 461).

Randy could find meaning in this prayer and pray it with a kind of joyous confidence because he had cultivated that confidence before his time of calamity.

How many persons I share with who don't have that confidence! It is only in calamity that they turn to the Lord. Now, to be sure, we *should* go to the Lord in a time of calamity. In fact, it's the only place to go. But we need to think carefully here. If God is not the shelter in the storm that God might be, it may be that we don't recognize God's presence. We need to remember that we can't count on God's relationship in trying times unless the relationship is cultivated when the storms are not raging.

The question is a relevant one: Does it take calamity to turn us to God? "When I am afraid," the psalmist said, "I put my trust in thee."

The Test of Trust

That leads us to a second consideration: True trust is tested only in the deep-down realities of life. That's the meaning of the image "Put thou my tears in thy bottle."

My friend Ellsworth Kalas is a remarkable preacher—one of the most effective preachers I know. He shares the fact that when he was a senior in high school and began to preach, affirmations were coming from everywhere. He became rather cocky. He seemed to be the pride of a lot of people.

One day a good man sat down and had an honest visit with Ellsworth, expressing truth with the kind of kindness that is hard to come by.

"Ellsworth," he said, "God has given you a good deal of talent, and you've been helping yourself, too, by studying your Bible. You preach surprisingly well—better than some full-time preachers. But I wouldn't want you for my pastor."

He paused for a moment and let those words sink in, until he could see that Ellsworth wanted to hear what he was going to say next.

"It's because you don't have any scars. You haven't been hurt enough to have real compassion. You've got the theory, but you don't have the pain to back it up. You'll be a different kind of preacher when you get some scars."

Some years later, Ellsworth says, he learned what the man meant. The gentle man was telling Ellsworth that he was a smart kid—perhaps even a smart-aleck kid—and that what he needed was to be tossed by storms until he was afraid for his life, until he cried desperately to God for mercy. Then perhaps he would preach better because his sermons would be delivered through pain and scars. Reflecting upon that, Ellsworth said, "Believe me, there is no substitute."

I agree with Ellsworth. True trust is tested only in the deep-down realities of life. That's a part of the meaning of the image "Put thou my tears in thy bottle."

Again, my brother-in-law, Randy, is a witness for us. (If you haven't read the introduction to this book, please do so now.) After the first round of heavy chemotherapy, Randy went into remission, and everything looked good. Then it struck again. We who have not experienced it can only faintly imagine the trauma of recurring malignancy.

I had sent Randy some sermons I had preached on this theme "Put thou my tears in thy bottle." I had affirmed that God not only knows our tossings and turnings, God cares. Randy responded with a beautiful witness about trust:

> I have grown to love the Psalms during this past year. It is true that God does know of all our tossings.
>
> And now I will share with you a prayer experience that proves this to me. It was a major experience with Jesus. Father Rick said I have been touched in a way few people ever experience.
>
> For several years I have prepared for prayer by going through a total relaxation phase to release my body and mind for prayer. After a few moments I travel in my mind to a place in the north Georgia mountains where I used to go on camping trips. There I have built an open structure, a gazebo, where I go to talk with Jesus. Normally I go in and call for Jesus and he comes in. We visit, and usually I give him my prayers of thanksgiving and intercessions. It's a conversational sort of setting.
>
> In late August, I was completely demoralized with the recurrence of the lymphoma. I was an emotional wreck; I went into prayer. Everything went on as normal until Jesus came to the door of the gazebo. At that moment a completely

unthought-of event happened that shook me to tears. I became like a camera recording the event. A little boy, me, when I was about Evan's age (five years), ran up to Jesus and hugged him. He picked me up and carried me to a seat and held me in his arms. He hugged me. I didn't say anything, but he knew my "tossings." He knew I was frightened. There were no answers and the future seemed so dim. As he hugged me he said, "Trust me. Trust me."

It was real, a personal miracle. He held me for a long time that night, until he knew I understood what he meant. I've told just a few people about this, and every time I tell it, even as I type this for you, tears come to my eyes; and the feeling I experienced that night renews itself in me. Rick said that feeling is "the same reason Moses couldn't look God in the face and why we remove our shoes on holy ground." And now I know that experience, too. We must trust Jesus as a child trusts—totally.

Because of this, whatever turns out to be the ultimate result of this disease, it's not the burden it was before. He made no promises, nor did he reveal the future, but he provided the format for living out the rest of my life with just two words . . . *Trust me.*

So, the psalmist could say, "When I am afraid, I put my trust in thee."

Gratitude in All Seasons

The third affirmation at which I want us to look is in verse 12: "My vows to thee I must perform, O God; I will render thank offerings to thee." The psalmist knew that gratitude is the virtue for all seasons. To be able to express gratitude—to be able to see reasons for being thankful—is to a marked degree the measure of any person.

The church I serve as senior minister in Memphis is thirty-six years old. The congregation has had only two other senior ministers: Dr. Charles W. Grant and Dr. Harold Beaty. Members of the congregation who have been in the church for a long time share exciting stories from these men's ministry. Both Doctors Grant and Beaty were outstanding preachers; people in the congrega-

81

tion remember them and talk about them, and that makes me happy.

One sermon Dr. Beaty preached has been mentioned a lot. He titled it "Life's Greatest Virtue." The first time someone mentioned it to me, I got a copy of it and read it. It was a sermon on gratitude. Dr. Beaty began that sermon by quoting Cicero, who said, "The grateful heart is not only the greatest virtue but mother of all the others." Then he went on to talk about individuals who are blinded by self-interest to the point that they miss the glories of God. He mentioned what Charles Lamb replied to a friend who said the world seemed "drained of all its sweets." "Drained of all its sweets? I don't know what you mean. Are there not roses and violets and the sun and moon reigning in the heavens?"

Then said Dr. Beaty, "Like the rest of us, Charles Lamb walked a mile with sorrow many times, yet he never forgot God's wonderful goodness."

The last point he made in his sermon on gratitude was this: "The grateful heart sees beneath the surface to the source of life's blessings." He illustrated his point in this fashion. Richard Cabot used to say to his students at Harvard:

> When you say to me, "thank you," remember I couldn't have done for you what I did, had not hundreds of others done for me. They could not have done for me what they did, had not thousands done for them. So the thing goes on in infinite time and space. Therefore, when you say thank you to anyone, you really are saying, "Thank you, God" (Beaty, December 30, 1979).

That is getting back to the Source. The Bible says God is the Alpha and the Omega—the Beginning and the End. Grateful persons think back to God, the Alpha, the beginning of all that is and ever will be. God is everything, and apart from God we are nothing.

How well Dr. Beaty knew what he was preaching about! When we know, in retrospect, what Dr. Beaty was going through, his words take on poignant and powerful meaning. His wife was emotionally ill, was hospitalized a number of times, and was constantly in emotional turmoil. Her emotional problems led to divorce, but Dr. Beaty continued to care for her as best he could. Then the tragedy happened. She shot him and then shot herself.

What a gracious person he was, how much in touch with the Source, even in the midst of what must have been the most trying, confusing, excruciatingly painful life a person could know. Maybe that was the source of his power. He prayed to God, "Put thou my tears in thy bottle."

His tears were not wasted. They turned Dr. Beaty into a gracious, tender man who loved without limits. He was a man of gratitude who never forgot to pay his vows and to render gratitude. He could thus say with the psalmist, "This I know, that God is for me."

I've not yet discovered the translation that Dr. Beaty used when he quoted Psalm 56 in that classic sermon on gratitude. But I want to find it. Verse 13 he rendered in this fashion: "For Thou hast delivered my soul from death: wilt not Thou deliver my feet from falling, that I may walk before God, living in the sunshine?"

That's the closing line of the psalm, and I'd like it to be the closing thought of this chapter. When God answers our prayer to put our tears in God's bottle, we can know that we can walk with God, living in the sunshine, despite the shadows that sometimes come our way.

PSALM 137

By the waters of Babylon, there we sat down and wept,
    when we remembered Zion.
On the willows there
    we hung up our lyres.
For there our captors
    required of us songs,
and our tormentors, mirth, saying,
    "Sing us one of the songs of Zion!"

How shall we sing the LORD'S song
    in a foreign land?
If I forget you, O Jerusalem,
    let my right hand wither!
Let my tongue cleave to the roof of my mouth,
    if I do not remember you,
if I do not set Jerusalem
    above my highest joy!

Remember, O LORD, against the Edomites
    the day of Jerusalem,
how they said, "Rase it, rase it!
    Down to its foundations!"

O daughter of Babylon, you devastator!
    Happy shall he be who requites you
    with what you have done to us!
Happy shall he be who takes your little ones
    and dashes them against the rock!

FIVE

SINGING THE LORD'S SONG IN A FOREIGN LAND

A few years ago when George Bush was serving as our vice president, he represented our country by attending the funeral service of Leonid Brezhnev. Brezhnev was the general secretary of the Soviet Union from 1964 to 1982. After Bush became president, he recalled this experience when talking about the necessity of faith for leadership in our country. He said very emphatically that he didn't believe a person could be president of the United States without faith in God. Then he added that he felt this faith was much more universal than we often think.

He shared an amazing thing that happened at the funeral of Brezhnev. Things were running to a military precision; a coldness and hollowness pervaded the ceremony. There were marching soldiers in steel helmets. There was an almost endless stream of Marxist rhetoric—but no prayers, no comforting hymns, no mention of God.

Mr. Bush said that, from where he was sitting, he was able to see Mrs. Brezhnev. She walked up to the casket, took one last look at her husband, and there in the cold, gray center of the totalitarian atheistic state, she appeared to trace the sign of the cross over her husband's chest.

The President said that he was stunned by that simple act, that God had broken through, even in the hollowness of that communist ceremony.

For me, it's a poignant picture of a suppressed faith exploding into expression. In the face of death, in her time of pain, I like to think that Mrs. Brezhnev could not keep her faith hidden. Perhaps that which was deep within, maybe kept secret for years in the arena of atheism where she lived her public life, now emerged, maybe even against her will.

PSALM 137: HOW SHALL WE SING IN A FOREIGN LAND?

We have another picture of almost the opposite phenomenon in Psalm 137. Here, there were people wanting to express their faith, but desperate as to how to do it. Get the setting in mind.

Babylon was like a prison for the children of Israel. They found themselves there, not as willing tourists, but as the unwilling spoils of battle. Jerusalem fell to Babylon in 587 B.C. Deportation followed immediately for a significant number of Judah's ablest and most productive citizens. They found themselves in exile in a land that had nothing but contempt for Yahweh.

When one of those exiles, upon his return years later, reflected on his experience, he wrote these words that are among the most touching in the Bible:

> By the waters of Babylon,
> there we sat down and wept,
> when we remembered Zion.
> On the willows there
> we hung up our lyres.
> For there our captors
> required of us songs,
> and our tormentors, mirth, saying,
> "Sing us one of the songs of Zion!"
> (Psalm 137:1-3)

Ernest T. Campbell suggests that some have imagined that the enslaving Babylonians, partying it up on Saturday night, had sought to compel the Hebrews to add to the merriment by singing their sacred songs. An invitation to such sacrilege, we may be sure, the Jews resisted. They were not about to cast their pearls before swine (Campbell, April 30, 1972).

There is a larger truth to this passage with which we need to grapple. The psalmist's question is a probing one: How shall we sing the Lord's song in a foreign land?

It's a question that we find ourselves asking now and again. But let's stay with Israel for a moment. Israel had long found help in the songs of the Lord. The Lord and his songs were identified with the land of Zion.

> But this new crisis called for something beyond the old ways of relating to God. How could the songs of Zion be sung in the land of those who had conquered Zion? God had been understood as Zion's God, yet Zion was far away. Could the God of the land of Zion be praised in the land of a victorious enemy far away? (Allen, p. 12).

This was a turning point—a crossroad for the Lord's people. They had to rethink who God was and who they were in relation to God. The Bible is filled with accounts of turning points in persons' lives. It happens over and over again in our lives. We come to a crossroad, a new situation, a circumstance or experience we have never engaged before, and we have to rethink our relationship to God. In other words, a static faith is not an adequate faith.

You remember how James Russell Lowell put it in the hymn "Once to Every Man and Nation":

> New occasions teach new duties
> Time makes ancient good uncouth;
> They must upward still and onward
> Who would keep abreast of truth.

A static faith is not a faith that will sustain us. In fact, a static faith really is no faith at all.

The Journey and Growth of Faith

There are two common and telling images for the Christian life—the image of the Christian life as a journey and the image of the Christian life as growth. These images are biblical ones. They give a foundation for understanding the place of spiritual crises, change, and dynamic in our lives.

Christians are believers in motion. The life of faith is a life of journey. One of the most popular books ever written in English is John Bunyan's *Pilgrim's Progress*. Written way back in 1678, it is still a great resource. It is the classic allegory of the spiritual life as a journey.

Abraham in the Old Testament is the model person to illustrate the image of journey—his whole life was spent journeying toward hope unseen. His story is told in two cryptic verses in Chapter 12 of Genesis. Verse 1: "Now the Lord said to Abram, 'Go from your country and your kindred and your father's house to the land that I will show you.' " Verse 4: "So Abram went, as the Lord had told him."

The writer of the letter to the Hebrews retold that story in this fashion: "By faith Abraham obeyed . . . and he went out, not knowing where he was to go. By faith he sojourned in the land of promise, as in a foreign land" (Heb. 11:8-9).

Abraham's descendants became the people of God who made that exodus journey, traveling through the wilderness toward the promised land. After living in the promised land for a time, the depth of the people's faith was measured as they faced another journey, the journey into the Babylonian exile. It was out of that exile experience that this probing question arose: "How shall we sing the Lord's song in a foreign land?"

The prophet Micah described the individual's relationship to God in terms of journey as well:

> He has showed you, O man, what is good;
>   and what does the Lord require of you
> but to do justice, to love kindness,
>   and to walk humbly with your God?
> (Micah 6:8)

It's the same in the New Testament. Believers were called to be followers of "the way." They were called "followers of the way" even before they were called Christians. To be sure, in the New Testament, this pointed to a way of life rather than to a literal road, but that does not lessen the impact of the image of disciples as followers, travelers, sojourners. These disciples are always moving, as Paul said, "from faith to faith" (Rom. 1:17, KJV).

The second key image or metaphor for Christian life is that of growth. The Christian's journey is growth toward maturity in Jesus Christ. The goal of the journey is mature personhood—to grow up in "the measure of the stature of the fulness of Christ" (Eph. 4:13).

Those images—journey and growth—speak clearly to my contention that a static faith is not an adequate faith. Our relationship with God must change as our understanding of God grows.

In the latter part of the psalm, there is a perfect illustration of the limitation of a static faith. Look at verses 8-9:

> O daughter of Babylon, you devastator!
>   Happy shall he be who requites you
>   with what you have done to us!
> Happy shall he be who takes your little ones
>   and dashes them against the rock!
>   (Psalm 137:8-9)

What is a passage like that doing in holy scripture? A man of God, a singer of Israel's songs in praise of God, relishing the thought that his enemies would be punished by having the heads of their children bashed against a stone. That's a long way—a galaxy away—from the prayer of our Lord on the cross: "Father, forgive them; for they know not what they do."

But that's not the only instance. Look specifically at Deuteronomy 21:18-21:

> If a man has a stubborn and rebellious son, who will not obey the voice of his father or the voice of his mother, and, though they chastise him, will not give heed to them, then his father and his mother shall take hold of him and bring him out to the elders of his city at the gate of the place where he lives, and they shall say to the elders of his city, "This our son is stubborn and rebellious, he will not obey our voice; he is a glutton and a drunkard." Then all the men of the city shall stone him to death with stones; so you shall purge the evil from your midst; and all Israel shall hear, and fear.

91

We could cite many references in the Old Testament that present an understanding of God foreign to what we see clearly revealed in Jesus Christ. I remember a story that E. Stanley Jones told about a mother who was reading to her little girl the Old Testament account of the massacre of the Amalekites. The little girl was bothered. She could not understand how the God who told us in Christ to love our enemies could approve of wholesale murder. So her mother told her that the people who lived back then did not know as much about God as we do—that now we have Christ. The little girl's face lighted up, and she said, "Oh, yes, Mother, now I see. Back then, God was not a Christian."

That makes the point. It's not that God was not a Christian. God was always like Jesus, because Jesus is God's presentation of God's self to us. But it's obvious that Old Testament scripture writers did not see God as the Gospel writers or Paul and other New Testament writers did. In the pages of the Bible, understanding of God changes as people come closer to the full revelation of God's character in Jesus Christ.

Perhaps you know the story about Gamaliel Bradford, who wrote a book on Robert E. Lee. When he began his book, he approached his subject in a spirit of hostility. He had little sympathy for the South—and that's putting it kindly. At first he decided that the title of his book would be *Lee the Rebel.* As he studied the material and came to know his man better, he decided that *rebel* was not quite the word he wanted. So he changed the working title to *Lee the Southerner.* After reading more and getting to know Lee still better, he decided that to call him a southerner was also inadequate. So, he changed the title to the one by which we know the book today: *Lee the American.*

So, how is the God, who is often seen in the Old Testament as vengeful, advising conduct that would turn even the stomachs of those who make no noble moral claims, the same God who came to be known as "our Father" in the Gospels?

What happened?

God did not change: "From everlasting to everlasting thou art God" (Psalm 90:2). What happened? Persons' understanding changed. A static faith is an inadequate faith.

92

Growing in Our Understanding of Scripture

Using the illustration of scripture itself, then, we are called to deal with one of the most perplexing issues confronting Christians in every age: our understanding and use of scripture. Great controversy swirls around the question of biblical authority and what that means. That battle of thought goes on within the church.

I was one of six United Methodist ministers who initiated *The Houston Declaration* that shaped to a marked degree the direction of the General Conference of United Methodism in 1986. The first issue of that declaration was the primacy of scripture. The new theological statement of The United Methodist Church, passed at that conference, underscores clearly—that the Bible is the word of God—that it is the primary and authoritative source for salvation, faith, and doctrine. In the Christian life and in Christian theology, scripture is primary and is our authority.

Well then, do we disregard the Old Testament and adhere only to the New? That might help in resolving conflict, but it would woefully limit God's witness. Neither would it solve the problem of authority, the nature of faith, and the primacy of the God's word. Even in the New Testament there are at least surface contradictions. So what do we do with the Bible? Let me offer five suggestions.

One, we commit ourselves to an understanding of God as revealed by Jesus. To know who God is and how God acts we look at Jesus Christ. Some unknown poet put it in this fashion:

> Here is truth in a little creed
> Enough for all the roads we go
> In love is all the law we need
> In Christ is all the God we know.

That's a pretty good summary. To know God and how God acts, we look at Jesus Christ.

Two, we interpret the word by the word. If there is an apparent contradiction in a specific section of scripture, we resolve the contradiction by looking at the context of the whole Bible.

Three, we look to the Bible not to close a discussion but to open one. I like the way William Sloane Coffin put it:

It is a mistake to sharpen our minds by narrowing them. . . . God leads with a light rein, giving us our head. Jesus told parables for this reason: stories have a way of shifting responsibility from the narrator to the hearer. Christians have to listen to the world as well as to the Word. And do not all of us learn more when we do not try to understand too soon? (Coffin, p. 7).

Four, we are to see the Bible not as a hitching post, but as a signpost. We can make an idol of the Bible, and people do that. Some people pay more attention to trying to define and refine dogma by a hidebound proof-text approach to scripture than they do to the living word for which scripture is a channel. Sometime ago I was in an ecumenical gathering that was both exciting and sad. It was exciting because powerful witness was being made to the transforming power of Jesus Christ. It was sad because a couple of people were hung up on what they labeled "purity of doctrine." Not only were they surprised to discover what they labeled as "born-again" Christians among us United Methodists, one of them made the arrogant claim that she had given her life to a quest for purity of doctrine. She said it as a kind of indictment against denominations other than her own.

"My Lord," I said to myself, "what an empty quest! That's what the Pharisees were about—pure doctrine."

The Bible is not about dogma; it's not about pure doctrine. It's not even about itself. The Bible never points to itself; it points to God. It is not concerned about words, but about the Word, the Living Word.

Don't get hung up on the wrong issues. It's true that scripture is a clear and authoritative witness. It's true that "God is love, and he who abides in love abides in God, and God abides in him" (1 John 4:16). If these statements are true, then revelation is in relationship—the relationship between Christ and us, and between others and us.

I heard of a young boy who was saying his prayers in New Haven. New Haven is the site of Yale University, and there are a lot of stereotypes about the arrogance abounding there. This little boy in New Haven prayed: "Our Father, who art in New Haven, how did you know my name?" Well, his words were mixed up; but in a very real sense, he was expressing in his own way exactly what our Christian faith does say to us. God is present with us wherever we are (even in New Haven) and God knows each of us personally by name. God so loved the world (and every person in it) that he gave his only son.

And that brings me to the last thing I want to say about the Bible. *The Bible is to be read as the story of the triumph of God's grace.* If we will remember that, we won't get stuck on issues that we don't fully understand yet. Rather, we will read on and stay with the story until the story, and we ourselves, are baptized in the light of God's grace shining brightly in Jesus Christ.

Kierkegaard said that most of us read the Bible the way a mouse tries to remove the cheese from the trap without getting caught. Some of us have mastered that. We read the story as though it were about someone else a long time ago; that way we don't get caught. But if we see the Bible as the story of the triumph of God's grace, the story of God searching for *us,* then look out. The story will come alive. God will find us and we will know that we are found. Then we will sing the Lord's song—at least we will try desperately to do so.

It's Not Easy to Sing the Lord's Song

Let's get back to the assertion that a static faith is not an adequate faith. We need a moving, growing faith as we are always finding ourselves in a strange land. It's a strange land in which we live. How do we sing the Lord's song?

In 1989, the first "embryo trial" in our nation took place in Maryville, Tennessee. It was a trial to decide the disposition of seven frozen embryos in dispute in the divorce case between Junior Davis and Mary Sue Davis.

"Mrs. Davis . . . wants to implant the pre-embryos in her uterus in an attempt to have children. Her husband doesn't understand why she wants to bear children in a failed marriage. He said he would never have consented to the fertilization procedure had he known he would file for divorce" (*The Commercial Appeal,* August 10, 1989).

The case of frozen embryos may be easy compared to the question of abortion, with the changing of the Supreme Court interpretation of laws and the passing of a new one. And that's not the end of it. The pill that is being perfected in France, RU-486, enables a woman to take it after intercourse to get rid of egg and sperm and never know whether she has conceived or not. What moral questions does this issue raise? What do we do with science and technology when they bring us to the place of human engineering and such easy control of life over death—and death over life? How do we sing the Lord's song in such a strange land?

It's not as easy as some would make it. There are a lot of gray areas in the arena of moral decisions.

When We Can't Even Sing

The truth is there are times when we can't sing the Lord's song. Most of us could tell of an experience when our throats went dry, our lips seemed parched, and our tongues were so heavy that we could not sing. There were no words of joy, no expressions of confident faith. God seemed to be nowhere about; God certainly seemed absent from *us*. Most of us could tell of some experience that was so painful, so disillusioning, so threatening to our faith that we couldn't sing the Lord's song. Some of us tried, but we couldn't. Some of us didn't even try—singing the Lord's song didn't even seem to be an option.

Maggie Savoy was a talented newspaper woman—society editor of *The Los Angeles Times*. She had undergone surgery for abdominal cancer and recovered. Then, five and a half years later, the disease struck again. From raw notes which were to become a book, United Press International issued excerpts which show how she felt and what she wanted to say.

> Dying is more beautiful the second time around.
> Not easier. But there is joy to be wrung from the second time. I messed up horrendously the first time—my script was flawed, my performance scrawny, resentful, hysterical, and terribly cruel to those I love and who love me. I know

my lines better now. I know a little more about the craft of dying.

First time around I couldn't find any help. As an outline, one does go through certain steps. They overlap, and not necessarily in order. Disbelief, it can't happen to me, calm, then rage and fury and debilitating feeling sorry for yourself.

Somewhere there comes a heightened sense of ME, and another rage that there will be NO me.

And then slowly, an entirely new value structure, especially time, possessions, and how to use your energies.

Like the fact of cancer, I learned another fact. I may not have the choice over what kills me, but I do have a choice over what I kill. I have the power to shape, make, spend, use every single hour still on the books. And I have the power to shape, make, and build love. These are the only things I really own, the only ME there is. Slowly, like a left-handed kid learns to write—I learned by practice: One has the power over the quality of one's life. That is all. (Shelby, "How Deep is Down?" February 25, 1973).

There are times when we can't sing—or we think we can't. And it doesn't help us to pretend. Don't lie about it. Be honest. Find someone, or a few persons, with whom you can share. Let them know the emptiness you feel, your pain, your sense of being betrayed. There is someone who will understand and who will listen and who will stick with you and accept your raging, your withdrawal, or your questioning silence. Don't try to sing when your singing is going to mock your feelings.

At the same time, don't give in to the despair. Don't let the experience of loss or pain or betrayal speak the last word. Not only Maggie Savoy, but countless other witnesses confirm the power that is always ours as human beings:

—"to shape, make, spend, and use every single hour still on the books";

—"to shape, make, and build love"

—to determine the quality of our life and our relationships.

When you add to that basic power of human life, the power of Christ and his indwelling presence, though we may not be able to sing now, the song will come again.

We Don't Sing Alone

Consider this final thought: Singing the Lord's song is not a solo performance. We sing together, or we sing for someone else until he or she can sing. Sometimes, others sing for us until our hearts are warmed and our tongues loosened, and we can join the singing.

Did you see the TV movie *The Women of Brewster Place*, starring Oprah Winfrey? I saw only a part of it and was inspired to read the book by Gloria Naylor. The movie and the book are gripping experiences.

I relished the book because of Gloria Naylor's powerful writing style. She paints portraits in words in a way that etches the personality not only in your mind but on your heart. You read the book and you feel you know the women of Brewster Place. Ms. Naylor delicately and accurately brings to life the agonies and triumphs of human beings born black and female.

One of the women is Mattie Michael. Mattie lived for her son, only to love him. She also lost her home because of his cowardice. But Mattie remained strong, bringing the power of love into the lives of others.

One of the other women of Brewster Place for whom Mattie kept singing the Lord's song was Etta Mae Johnson. She was Mattie's long-time friend who had lived off her beauty and her men all her life. But she was too old for that kind of life now; she came to Brewster Place, and Mattie took her in. But she tried to return to her old way of life one more time and got involved with a preacher, thinking that she had found someone with whom she could settle down for life. But he was the stereotypical charlatan, using others, especially women, for his own selfishness.

After a night out with him, discovering that he was no different from the rest, Etta was returning home to Mattie. The author tells the story:

> Etta removed her hat and massaged her tight forehead. Then, giving a resigned sigh, she started slowly down the street. Had her neighbors been out on their front stoops, she could have passed through their milling clusters as anonymously as the night wind. They had seen her come down that street once in a broken Chevy that had about five hundred

dollars' worth of contraband liquor in its trunk, and there was even the time she'd come home with a broken nose she'd gotten in some hair-raising escapade in St. Louis, but never had she walked among them with a broken spirit. This middle-aged woman in the wrinkled dress and wilted straw hat would have been a stranger to them.

When Etta got to the stoop, she noticed there was a light under the shade at Mattie's window, and she strained to hear what actually sounded like music coming from behind the screen. Mattie was playing her records! Etta stood very still, trying to decipher the broken air waves into intelligible sound, but she couldn't make out the words. She stopped straining when it suddenly came to her that it wasn't important what song it was—someone was waiting up for her. Someone who would deny fiercely that there had been any concern—just a little indigestion from them fried onions that kept me from sleeping. Thought I'd pass the time by figuring out what you see in all this loose-life music.

Etta laughed softly to herself as she climbed the steps toward the light and the love and the comfort that awaited her (Naylor, pp. 73-74).

Singing the Lord's song is not a solo performance. We sing together, or we sing for someone else until he or she can sing. Others sing for us until our hearts are warmed and our tongues loosened, and we can join the singing.

PSALM 24

The earth is the LORD'S and the fulness thereof,
    the world and those who dwell therein;
for he has founded it upon the seas,
    and established it upon the rivers.

Who shall ascend the hill of the LORD?
    And who shall stand in his holy place?
He who has clean hands and a pure heart,
    who does not lift up his soul to what is false,
    and does not swear deceitfully.
He will receive blessing from the LORD,
    and vindication from the God of his salvation.
Such is the generation of those who seek him,
    who seek the face of the God of Jacob. *Selah*

Lift up your heads, O gates!
    and be lifted up, O ancient doors!
    that the King of glory may come in.
Who is the King of glory?
    The LORD, strong and mighty,
    the LORD, mighty in battle!
Lift up your heads, O gates!
    and be lifted up, O ancient doors!
    that the King of glory may come in.

Who is this King of glory?
    The LORD of hosts,
    he is the King of glory! *Selah*

PSALM 127

Unless the LORD builds the house,
    those who build it labor in vain.
Unless the LORD watches over the city,
    the watchman stays awake in vain.
It is in vain that you rise up early
    and go late to rest,
eating the bread of anxious toil;
    for he gives to his beloved sleep.

Lo, sons are heritage from the LORD,
    the fruit of the womb a reward.
Like arrows in the hand of a warrior
    are the sons of one's youth.
Happy is the man who has
    his quiver full of them!
He shall not be put to shame
    when he speaks with his enemies in the gate.

SIX

HOW MAY WE COME TO GOD?

*A*lmost without fail, when my wife and I go to visit my parents down in Perry County, Mississippi, we will come around to talking about the Bible. Mutt (his name is Murdoc, but I call him Mutt, affectionately), my father, has his Bible by the recliner. He spends at least fifteen hours a day in that recliner, and he reads a lot. Other than watching all the game shows on TV, some of the soaps, and a lot of sports, that's about all Mutt does. He reads. Co-Bell (her name is Cora, but I call her Co-Bell, affectionately), my mother, doesn't read much. She says her eyes are not too good, and she's right; but I have a hunch she just doesn't like to read, and she gets plenty of jabs in at Mutt as he reads the daily paper, the weekly *Baptist Record,* and *Time* magazine from cover to cover. But, like Mutt, Co-Bell reads the Bible—especially the Psalms.

PSALM 24: WHO SHALL ASCEND THE HILL OF THE LORD?

For the past couple of years now, we've not gotten into conversation about the Bible without Co-Bell picking up her large-print edition off the coffee table and announcing, "This is my favorite scripture." It doesn't matter that she has shared that on our previous four or five visits—I'm not even sure if she remembers she has shared it. She gets joy and strength in reading it to me. In her choppy reading style—never cultivated for public reading—she begins her reading of the Twenty-Fourth Psalm: "The earth is the Lord's and the fulness thereof."

She will not stop until she has read at least through verses 3 and 4.

> The earth is the Lord's and the fulness thereof,
>   the world and those who dwell therein;
> for he has founded it upon the seas,
>   and established it upon the rivers.
> Who shall ascend the hill of the Lord?
>   And who shall stand in his holy place?
> He who has clean hands and a pure heart,
>   who does not lift up his soul to what is false,
>   and does not swear deceitfully.

And always—it never fails—she stops at that point in her reading, and says to me with earnest conviction, "Son, I've got clean hands and a pure heart."

It's one of those rituals of home and parents that adds stoutness to my soul. Intuitively, Mom knows this is a great psalm, a premier piece of scripture. It wouldn't matter to Co-Bell, but it may to us, that this psalm is a festival hymn, perhaps 2,500 years old. The words, however, hearken back to Israel's struggles and victories after the settlement of Palestine. The verses that are preserved in the present psalm are fragments and antiphons taken from what is called a liturgy.

In your imagination, see the bedraggled but triumphant army of Israel, returning from battle. In their battles, Israel's army carried the ark of the covenant with them. The ark was the visible dwelling of the invisible God. To know that God was with them gave the people courage and confidence.

After the battle and the victory, the ark was brought back to the sanctuary. So, one of the settings of this psalm must have been a priestly procession and a military parade, celebrating God's war heroes as they returned from victory. When the ark arrived at Zion, there was a kind of liturgy, a ceremonial game of question and answer between those who had returned from battle and the people who were awaiting them. Those at the gate to the city would shout. "Who shall ascend the hill of the Lord? And who shall stand in his holy place?" The response would come clear, "He who has clean hands and a pure heart" (Psalm 24:3-4).

"Who is the King of glory?" The response would come, "The Lord, strong and mighty, the Lord, mighty in battle!" (Psalm 24:8).

"Lift up your heads, O gates! and be lifted up, O ancient doors!" would come the shout. The response: "that the King of glory may come in" (Psalm 24:9).

Then the procession moved into the holy city, and the great celebration began.

That was the original setting. Now, the psalm lives on, recited by faithful Jews as the first act of awakening on the first day of each week. It is used by liturgical Christians worldwide on what we call Ascension Day. Many churches in the Reformed tradition sing verses 7 through 9 before Holy Communion.

My mom, Co-Bell, down in Perry County, Mississippi, who knows nothing about ritual or liturgy, and probably would not know the meaning of either word, has been touched by this word, which for 2,500 years has taught people the absolute priority of God in their lives.

Who Is the King of Glory?

Notice first, as is almost always the case, the psalm begins and ends with God. Relish for a moment the way the psalmist talks about God: "The earth is the Lord's and the fulness thereof, the world and those who dwell therein" (Psalm 24:1). Live for a moment with the title the psalmist gives to God: "The King of glory." This God is not merely Israel's war hero. God is the King of glory, the Lord of all the countries of the world. The splendor of God's glory will bless all nations with righteousness.

Do you spend much time thinking about God? Even if we do, most of our thinking is vague, isn't it? Hardly ever do we just sit and reflect on the nature of God. Think about it; our God is "the King of glory."

Our day isn't one that makes it easy to think in terms of the transcendent, omnipotent, omniscient God. We've taken control of the universe—so we think. We see ourselves as "kings of glory."

> At the time when the psalm was written, human beings were small, and nature was great and mysterious. In the sands of the desert, the storms, the times of drought and the periods of flood, nature was not subject to human beings; human beings were at the mercy of nature. As a result, petty humanity saw sinister gods and demons at work in the mighty forces of nature. And yet Israel acknowledged Yahweh as creator, trusted in the goodness of his creation, and did not allow itself to be intimidated (Moltmann, pp. 21-22).

So this is no poetic word born in the imagination of a singer of Israel. This is the experience of Israel's people. Our God is the King of glory, the Lord of hosts, they sang. Many people today do not acknowledge God as the King of glory. We learn from our culture that we can be or do anything if we try hard enough. But is trying hard really enough?

I think of the experience of Tom Monaghan, founder of Domino's Pizza and owner of the Detroit Tigers. He grew up in an orphanage in Jackson, Michigan, back in the early forties. He wanted to be a shortstop for the Detroit Tigers, a priest, and an architect. He didn't become a priest or an architect, but he made it to the Tigers; he became the owner of the team.

The person who was really special to him in that orphanage was Sister Mary Berarda. She was kind and caring, lively and full of encouragement. She would say to him often, "OK, Tom. Have faith in God, have faith in yourself—then go out and do it! You can be anything you want to be."

She showed up at every game he was in, started him reading books—a mighty important contribution to his life—and was a steady influence for good in his life.

But after he became a big success, he forgot all about Sister Mary. Then one day the Toastmasters organization asked if he would give a speech on the person who most influenced his life.

The first name that popped up in his head was Sister Mary

Berarda. He sought to find her but heard she had died. He felt ashamed—ashamed that he had forgotten for so long this woman who had meant so much to him. Later, he found out she had not died. He found out where she was and went to see her. She was in a wheelchair. Her face was lined with wrinkles. Despite her age, her eyes danced and shone with the kindness he remembered so well.

Tom said, "I did what you said, Sister. I followed your advice; I had faith in myself. I'm a self-made man."

"Yes, you're successful," she said. "And I always knew you could do it. But, Tom, there really is no such thing as a self-made man." Then she pressed her most precious possession, her rosary, into his hand.

The more he thought about it, the more he realized she was right. God was the source of his life, and he had not put God first in his life.

And so with too many of us. We need to experience the truth of the exhilarant shout of the psalmist, "The Lord of Hosts, he is the King of glory!" God is our Lord and our King.

Clean Hands and a Pure Heart

The psalmist begins and ends with God—but in between he talks about us humans. So we ask the question, how are we to come to God?

Two things make us fit or unfit to stand in God's holy place: our actions and our attitudes. Those who have "clean hands," the psalmist says—that has to do with our actions, what we do. And those who have a "pure heart"—that has to do with our attitudes, how we feel.

Put another way, I don't think it has as much to do with our performance as it has to do with our will and with our willingness. The question is not "Have you kept the law?" or "Have you performed the required sacrifices?" but "Do you have clean hands and a pure heart?"

Entry into the presence of God and relationship with God is dependent upon our desire—the sincerity of our purpose—not the success of our performance.

I think of another modern saint, also a Roman Catholic and a woman—Mother Teresa. She is one of my heroes. I met her once, though briefly. She came to Memphis, and my friend, Bishop Daniel M. Buechlein, invited me to the Mass celebrating the ministry of her order in our city. My wife, Jerry, and I had the opportunity of shaking hands with her, looking into those deep, compassionate eyes, and having her speak a simple word of blessing as we received a prayer medal from her. I'm currently carrying this medal in my pocket as a call to prayer and as a reminder of Mother Teresa's challenge to me, and to all of us. It's a challenge of agape love—total self-giving love—service to the poorest of the poor, who can give nothing in return, save their love.

If anyone is motivated by prayer in her relationships, it's Mother Teresa. We think of her ministry as one of service, but behind that is a life of prayer. And if you asked her about her ministry, she would talk as much about prayer as she would about service.

One of the most amazing things to me was what happened to those eight or nine thousand people when Mother Teresa and her nuns entered the coliseum where the Mass was celebrated. It was amazing to me, because I set it in contrast to what usually happens in that coliseum. I'm a basketball fan, and I go to all the basketball games I can. I've also attended concerts at the coliseum, and, at either event, it's bedlam—applause, screaming, yelling. It's the ultimate in noisy, enthusiastic response to what's going on. But when Mother Teresa and her nuns came out on the floor of that coliseum, a holy hush descended upon that crowd. The only thing you could hear was the nuns walking on the floor. Had they not been walking, you could have heard a pin drop. It was a kind of eerie hush that spoke of reverence and awe. This stoop-backed, wrinkled, tiny woman evoked a holy hush from that mass of people.

I know that this response happened because of what people know about her and her ministry—but I can't help but believe it's also a response to her very person. She is humility incarnate. Throughout that two-hour Mass she was in prayer. For a good part of the time, she was completely removed from what was going on around her. She buried her face in her hands and rested her elbows on her knees and cradled her head in deep prayer.

After the Mass, she spoke. She spoke simply, but her words penetrated the conscience of the audience because her words flowed out of a life of prayer and service. She called us to prayer and to a life of tender mercy—which she would say are inseparable. She punctuated her brief talk with some personal experiences. She told of walking on the streets of Calcutta and seeing something moving in a ditch. She had to look carefully to see that it was an emaciated man, still alive, but covered with worms. She took him back to their center that cares for the dying. She said it took them three hours to pick the worms off the man, to clean him up, to give him a bath, to give him some simple food, and to introduce him to love—love and prayer with no strings attached.

The man died. But he died with dignity, knowing that he was loved. Demonstrating this kind of love is the real ministry of Mother Teresa and her Sisters. As he lay dying, he looked up at Mother Teresa and said, "I lived like an animal on the streets, but I am going to die as an angel, loved and cared for." And he smiled as he died.

To be sure, that's dramatic; our days will not be filled with that kind of dramatic story. Neither are Mother Teresa's. But her days are filled with responsive love to the people she meets because she is motivated by prayer.

At the Mass, Bishop Francis Stafford, former Roman Catholic bishop in Memphis, preached the homily. He told of having been with Mother Teresa a few weeks earlier. They were walking along an enclosed cloister in a convent where they were together for a retreat. They were in silence. Mother Teresa stopped for a long time before a statue of the crucified Christ, and he could hear her whispering in earnest prayer: "I thirst . . . I thirst . . . I thirst."

In that snapshot of this saint of God, Bishop Stafford said he discovered her secret. It is her desire—her burning thirst for more of Christ.

So being with God, and being God's people, is a matter of will and willingness. "Who shall ascend to the hill of the Lord? And who shall stand in his holy place? He who has *clean hands*" (Psalm 24:3-4). Let's look at our hands.

Certainly they are not clean. They were clenched when they should have been open. They have fended others off when they might have invited. They seized and snatched when they should have given. They struck and condemned and took possession when they should have yielded. Our hands are not clean.

"Who shall ascend to the hill of the Lord? And who shall stand in his holy place? He who has clean hands and a *pure heart.*" Let's look at our hearts. Certainly, they can hardly be called pure. They are divided, torn hither and thither. They are full of fear and aggression. That is why we do not know what we live by and what we ought to do. We are confused. That is why we do not see God.

> We do not love with our whole hearts, and do not seek God with our whole hearts. With us, everything is half-hearted and divided. We accuse ourselves—and defend ourselves. And the worst thing of all is that when our hearts accuse us, we no longer know that God is greater than our hearts. That is why we continually reproach ourselves and other people" (Moltmann, pp. 25-26).

That's the reason we are guilt-stricken. Our hearts are not pure. Well, how can they be? If our hands are not clean and our hearts are not pure, will the gate open?

The centerpiece of Psalm 24 is the gate—the ancient doors to the city. I believe there is a door like that in your life and mine, and that door will be opened by our desire—our will and our willingness. We are driven back to will and willingness. What is our deepest desire?

Now this doesn't get us off the hook. The emphasis remains that we must have clean hands—right actions and pure hearts—right attitudes. We are not freed from the commitment and discipline of acting rightly as God would have us act, and feeling with love as God would have us feel; but we don't do it for merit. We do it because our deep desire is to be with God. We are judged by God not on the basis of how well we measure up, how absolutely clean our hands are, or how absolutely pure our hearts may be. We are judged according to our will and our willingness.

In Franz Kafka's great novel, *The Trial,* there is a parable of a man who is told to enter a kingdom through a certain gate. When he arrives at the edge of the kingdom, sure enough, he finds the gate there just as he was promised. He also finds a sentinel there—guarding the entrance. So, seeing the sentinel, he sits down on the grass outside, and he waits for the sentinel to either give him instructions or to grant him permission to enter. But the sentinel does nothing; he doesn't say anything or do anything. He just stands there at the gate.

The man continues to wait and wait. The days go by. Then the weeks. The months go by, and then the years. For a whole lifetime the fellow just sits there, and the sentinel just stands there. Finally one day, the sentinel leaves his post. He goes over to the big door, takes hold of it, closes it, and locks it. Before disappearing, he turns to the man out on the grass and says, "That door was made for you and for you alone. I was guarding it so that no one but you would enter. But because you chose not to enter it, it is now being closed forever!"

Sometimes the doors in our lives will only be opened by our willingness to go through them.

PSALM 127: THE LORD BUILDS THE HOUSE

I titled this chapter "How May We Come to God?" I don't mean an initial coming—or, our conversion. I mean how may we come to God in our ongoing relationship with God, in our ongoing covenant? Psalm 127 to which we turn now, speaks to that. It has the feel of Psalm 24, though it is in a different category. Psalm 24 is a "procession" hymn; Psalm 127 is one of a collection called "Songs of Ascents." This collection includes Psalms 120–134, fifteen in all. Literally, the meaning is "Songs for the Way Up" to Jerusalem. This little collection of songs, therefore, is a book of devotions for those "on *aliyah*" (pilgrimage) to Jerusalem. Interestingly, the same word is used today for the ingathering, the "coming up," of Jews to the modern state of Israel.

Most of us know this psalm by the first verse. It's among the most familiar and most quoted lines in the Psalter. Its Latin form, *nisi Dominus frustra*, has been quoted down through the centuries. It is the motto of one of my favorite, and one of the most beautiful, cities in all the world—Edinburgh, Scotland. That first verse is this: "Unless the Lord builds the house, those who build it labor in vain."

At first reading, that verse appears to be the emphasis of the psalm—the involvement of God in the community life of people. The psalm was probably written after the second exodus of Israel from Babylonian captivity. After their return, they got around to rebuilding their city and the temple, starting in about 520 B.C. That's the date we get from the book of Haggai. So, the psalm was probably written at the time of the rebuilding of the temple and the city.

Note the ordering of the first verse. *House* is mentioned before *city*.

> Unless the Lord builds the house,
>   those who build it labor in vain.
> Unless the Lord watches over the city,
>   the watchman stays awake in vain.
> (Psalm 127:1)

House, here, refers to the house of the Lord. For Israel, that was the dynamic center of community life—the house of the Lord. Wouldn't it be something if we could recover that dynamic in our day—the churches of our land becoming the nerve center, the heartbeat, the conscience of community life?

There is a family emphasis too. Though *house* is talking about the temple, when you get to verse 3, the emphasis is definitely on the family, on a house with children: "Lo, sons are a heritage from the Lord, the fruit of the womb a reward."

In the faith of Israel, people knew that without the Lord, they were not able to produce a family. To be sure, they could have children—a group of individuals quarreling, disconnected, rebellious. But they knew that children are the heritage of the Lord, that we receive them from the Lord as the Lord's gift to us and we take responsibility for them in that fashion. The creation of a happy family is God's will for humankind. Verse 5 speaks of the blessing that children are: "Happy is the man who has his quiver full of them!"

God Gives Us Sleep

The apparent emphasis of the psalm is the necessary involvement of God in the community life of people and in the family. But there's something else here that grabs my attention, and it's focused in the second part of verse 2: "For he gives to his beloved sleep."

The psalm is about trust, about the overcoming of anxiety. Look at the first part of verse 2: "It is in vain that you rise up early and go late to rest, eating the bread of anxious toil." This psalm speaks of the whole matter of anxiety and trust, the matter of our covenant relationship with God, and of how we come to God in our ongoing relationship with God. Here is a beautiful image of the rest God gives: God's gift of sleep.

Even when you think of it in a literal sense, it is a gift. My notion is that sleep is an important subject that deserves more attention than it gets. As a physiological phenomenon, sleep is an intriguing business. It involves us all. As Shelley put it, "Whatever moves, or toils, or grieves, hath its appointed sleep."

We spend sizable portions of our lives asleep—the child one-half its time, the adult one-third, and some elderly persons come to the point of doing little else but eating and sleeping. In sleep we let the windows of our eyes fall and steep our senses in forgetfulness.

Ernest T. Campbell has made some interesting observations about physical sleep:

> In sleep the nervous system becomes inactive. The brain is protected from the streams of impressions flowing from the sense organs. The pulse beats less frequently. We breathe less often. The gastric and peristaltic movements are less rapid. The pupils of the eyes contract. . . .
>
> The ability to sleep is a boon without price. Prolonged insomnia can wreck the nervous system and severely alter the disposition. Sleep is never more appreciated than when it eludes us. Like vitamin C, sleep cannot be stored up. Some animals can hibernate, but man cannot. He lives in a daily rhythm of work and rest. . . . For the man who trusts in the Almighty, sleep is a gift from God. The psalmist spoke it for us all when he said, "He giveth his beloved sleep" (Campbell, "The Gift of Sleep," March 5, 1972).

I'm emphasizing the physiology of sleep deliberately. However, this is not a lesson in physiology but a lesson in faith. I speak about the wonders of God's creation and our dependence upon God's natural gifts. As Campbell says, we do not *achieve* sleep, we *receive* it.

We need to recognize that and rejoice. We need to add sleep to our list of gifts for which we say thanks before we sleep at night.

With that word about literal sleep, let's look at sleep as the metaphor for resting in the Lord, for reflecting on our covenant relationship, for our ongoing coming to the Lord.

One thing that we need to remember about sleep is that it is God's way of reminding us of who is in command. We sleep every day—we come to the point when our energy diminishes, we can't keep our eyes open, and we have to give in to sleep.

> We must cut out, relinquish command, drop everything, release control, become totally disengaged, deny the world our brain and brawn—and entrust the management of history to our brethren who have already had their sleep and to God our keeper who slumbers not nor sleeps" (Campbell, March 5, 1972).

It's an important lesson to remember who is in command, to always know that we are God's servants, not gods ourselves. We're always forgetting that, aren't we?

Some years ago, General Omar Bradley boarded a commercial plane for a long trip. He was wearing a business suit, rather than his usual military attire. He found his assigned seat and began working on some important papers. Ironically, the general's seatmate turned out to be a private in the United States Army, and this young private was rather gregarious. He didn't recognize General Bradley, so he said to him, "Sir, we're going to be traveling together for some time. I think it would be nice if we got to know one another. I'm guessing that you are a banker."

Bradley, not wanting to be rude but wanting to get some work done, replied, "No, I'm not a banker. I'm General Omar Bradley, a Five-Star General in the United States Army. I'm head of the Joint Chiefs of Staff at the Pentagon in Washington, D.C."

After a slight pause, the young soldier said, "Well, Sir, that's a very important job. I sure hope you don't blow it."

When we remember that God is in control, we can have confidence because we know God is not going to blow it. When we receive the gift of sleep, we remember that we are God's servants, and that God is in control.

Now this suggestion: Sleep reminds us that we need to remember that we are not called to carry the whole world in our minds or on our hearts all the time. Accept the promise: "He gives to his beloved sleep." It's all right to "cut out" now and then! God made provision for our not being "on duty" all the time.

If anyone is an activist, I am. I have to discipline myself to be reflective, to claim and use solitude. I work about seventy hours a week. I need to hear this word—that I don't have to carry all the world in my mind or on my heart all the time.

The truth is, we do not seize the kingdom of God by our efforts. The kingdom of God is *bestowed.* It is not ours to take; it is God's to give. Jesus said, "Fear not, little flock, for it is your Father's good pleasure to give you the kingdom" (Luke 12:32). Overarching all other truths is this: We are to trust God to give us sleep; that is, we are to rest in God.

I read a story about a man who boarded an airplane one day. The fog on the ground was thick and heavy. With obvious apprehension, the man held on tensely as the plane taxied down the runway and lifted off. Higher and higher the pilot climbed, through what seemed to be an endless fog. Finally the plane broke through the top of the cloud—the fog bank—into the bright, clear sunshine. A man sitting next to the one telling the story leaned over and said quietly, "I suppose we can see clearly on any day that we gain enough altitude."

Though it's mixing figures of speech, these two images say the same thing. When we trust God to give us sleep—God gives us sleep. And it's in resting in God, in receiving God's gift of sleep, that we rise to that altitude where we can see things clearly.

Again, my brother-in-law, Randy, speaks to this. In the first months of his battle with cancer, before the possibility of a bone-marrow transplant was mentioned, when little or no hope was being offered for his healing, he wrote:

> Life has its highs and lows . . . the loss of a beloved family member, an illness, even financial setbacks. But our family has always held together in a way I have seen seldom in this

late part of the twentieth-century. Too often people just throw in the towel. Society has made that an easy way out. Just divorce or bankrupt or walk away from it. But there is great joy to meet the challenge, because I know that we are not alone. We won't be alone when we work together and help when help is needed.

Last night, Nancy was sitting in the chair beside my bed, exhausted from all she had done during the day . . . and week . . . and month. I remembered how I had sat in a chair beside her bed years before. What held us together then, as now, was love, pure love . . . just being able to help. Well, you have done the same for us—and it is a healing type of help. Every day, with every prayer, with every laugh, with every enactment of the lymphobusters, I feel healing taking place.

I can see there are many areas in my life that need healing—not just my physical self. As the prayer of confession points out sins of omission as well as commission, I have repeatedly neglected parts of my family life and not kept Nancy informed like I should about the state of the business. I believe that was a contributory factor to my illness . . . just the stress of containing those problems within me so as not to look weak or less than successful. Interesting how God has a way of taking care of those things for you, eventually. For example, "You can't drive for a year." Now that's a loss of late twentieth century American freedom! But although I have to regroup and coordinate drivers, a lot of the pressure is off. . . . I am having Nancy now balance our personal checking accounts and write checks to pay our bills. Now, she may still scream that we need more money, but she will know, for the first time since we've been married, how much our lifestyle costs! She can help choose whom to pay this month or what to cut out—and I can spend more time making money!

In any event, I feel healing. . . . It may have taken a major, catastrophic, almost terminal illness to bring this about, but all will be so much better soon. I know that when the tests are taken at the end of all this, the airborne and ground forces will have blown out every last lymphocyte in my body. But the healing will be deeper than even that. There will be full reconciliation within my spirit and soul such as I have never enjoyed before.

I truly feel the words written in *The Book of Common Prayer* in Reconciliation:

"Now there is rejoicing in heaven; for you were lost, and are found; you were dead, and are now alive in Christ Jesus our Lord. Go in peace. The Lord has put away all your sins. Thanks be to God" (1979 Edition, p. 451).

Randy had received God's gift of sleep, was resting in God, and had risen to that altitude of spirit where we can see things clearly.

Review what I've said about sleep:

One, in a very literal sense, sleep is a gift of God, and we are called to use it gratefully.

Two, sleep is God's way of reminding us in a concrete fashion who is in control.

Three, sleep stirs us to remember that we are not called to carry the whole world in our minds or on our hearts all the time.

Four, we are to trust God to give us sleep—we are to rest in the Lord.

Professor Donald Francis Toney often said to his students at Edinburgh that in music the rests are just as important as the notes. At first that appears to be an exaggeration, but musicians tell me that a choral or orchestra director soon learns that without careful attention to pause, the music will lose much of its beauty. So in the music of life, the *rests* must be written into the score. That's the way we keep coming in trust to God. We deliberately wait on the Lord to receive the gift of sleep. We go from our sleep with clean hands and a pure heart.

PSALM 23

The LORD is my shepherd, I shall not want;
 he makes me lie down in green pastures.
He leads me beside still waters;
 he restores my soul.
He leads me in paths of righteousness
 for his name's sake.

Even though I walk through the valley
  of the shadow of death,
 I fear no evil;
for thou art with me;
 thy rod and thy staff,
 they comfort me.

Thou preparest a table before me
 in the presence of my enemies;
thou anointest my head with oil;
 my cup overflows.
Surely goodness and mercy shall follow me
 all the days of my life;
and I shall dwell in the house of the LORD
 for ever.

SEVEN

IN THE HOUSE OF
THE LORD FOREVER

I had preached for thirty years before I ever preached a sermon on the Twenty-Third Psalm.

I have quoted it at funerals and weddings. I have shared it as comfort with sick folk. I don't know how many times I have laid my hands on the forehead of a dying person when that person was beyond conversation, stooped close, and whispered in his ear this psalm. I was certain sometimes, and praying hopefully at other times, that this pristine word of faith would be heard in the heart and be a balm of grace and a strong and comforting guide through the valley of the shadow of death.

The psalm had been in my repertoire of teaching, praying, sharing, counseling, and healing, but I had never preached a sermon on it. This psalm seemed to me to be the holy of holies of the psalms, and I've questioned my right and worthiness to enter its quiet, yet power-charged precinct. Also, how would I comment on such a thing of beauty? There are some things to which a word response is presumptuous, sometimes even sacrilege.

Apart from all that, my feelings of inadequacy about preaching on this sermon made me stay away from this psalm as a centerpiece for a sermon. But I broke my sermon silence in 1989, and now I am so bold as to make this "nightingale of the Psalms" the source of reflection for this last chapter.

The Lord Is My Shepherd

Let's begin by asking, Who is the Lord? How we think about God is critically important to our existence. We have reflected on the question implicitly throughout the previous chapters. Now, let's be explicit. Who is the Lord?

We can't quarrel with William Temple's observation:

> If your conception of God is radically false, then the more devout you are, the worse it will be for you. You're opening your soul to be molded by something base. You had much better be an atheist (Temple, p. 85).

We often think of God as being opposite from what we are. We are weak; God must be almighty. We are foolish; God must be all-wise. We are sinful, so God must be all-holy.

Then horribly, sometimes, we think of God as one who is and does what we would be and do if we were God! Destroy the enemy—why not? Perform a miracle to make people believe. Eliminate the opposition, if need be. We expect God to do what seems most logical to our minds, and we don't understand when God seems to behave otherwise.

Then into our limited and often distorted thinking comes the psalmist to cut our feet from under our overly ponderous way of thinking, to take our religious breath away by the simplicity of this statement: "The Lord is my shepherd."

There has been some scholarly debate about who wrote the psalm. But, for me, as F. B. Meyer says, "David's autograph is on every verse." Meyer has said it so well:

> But when and where did it first utter itself upon the ear of man? Was it sung first amid the hills of Bethlehem, as the sheep were grazing over the wolds, dotting them like chalk-stones? Or was it poured first upon the ear of the moody king, whose furrowed brow made so great a contrast to the fresh and lovely face of the shepherd-lad "who was withal of a beautiful countenance, and godly to look to"? . . . There is a strength, a maturity, a depth, which are not wholly compatible with tender youth, and seem rather to betoken the touch

of the man who has learnt good by knowing evil, and who, amid the many varied experiences of human life, has fully tested the shepherd-graces of the Lord of whom he sings. These words were surely first sung by one who had suffered deeply; who had tasted many a bitter cup; who had often been compelled to thread his way through many a dangerous labyrinth and beneath many an overhanging, low-browed rock.

David the king did not forget David the shepherd boy. There was a chamber in his heart whither he was wont to retire to meditate and pray; and there it was that he composed this Psalm, in which the mature experience of his manhood blends with the vivid memory of a boyhood spent among the sheep (Meyer, pp. 6-8).

Only David could have said so convincingly, "The Lord is my shepherd." Could there be a more descriptive way to bring our thinking down to earth, to put our minds and hearts into the right attitude to receive the grace of the Lord's being? What a picture: "The Lord is my shepherd."

Press the image now: "The Lord *is* my shepherd." It's a positive statement in the present tense. That's worth a long pause for reflection. We have a present-tense Lord. This impacts our lives completely. It certainly impacts our praying. The psalmist is not beseeching God to be something or do something. As Leslie Weatherhead says:

He is stating positively that he *is* and *does* all that is required by man. The writer does not say: Oh Lord, be my Shepherd! Make me to lie down in green pastures: lead me beside the still waters. He is asserting these very things and glorying in them. There is a place for petition, of course. Our Lord taught us to say, "Give us daily our bread for the coming day" (Matt. 6:11). But how magnificent it is to find in a Psalm written more than two thousand years ago, these calm assertions of trust! . . .

So many times we pray, asking that God will give something, when all that is necessary is that we should take something. After all, if God will not give, we cannot get, and if He will give, we have only to take (Weatherhead, pp. 20-21).

We remember this as we build our prayer life. We are God's children; why should we act like orphans? We don't have to convince the Lord to *be* our shepherd—God *is* our shepherd.

Press the image even further: "The Lord is *my* shepherd."

Someone has well said that "the heart of religion lies in its personal pronouns." What a difference that one little word, *my*, makes: *my* shepherd.

That's an affirmation of relationship. It defines the difference between knowing something and appropriating the knowledge into experience. It has to do with status—our status in relation to God.

Do you know your status as a child of God? Three men were talking about what status means. They asked, "How do you know when you have arrived?" The first man said, "I'll tell you what real status is. It's being invited to the White House for a personal conversation with the president." The second man said, "No, that's not it. You know you have status when you're invited to the White House for a personal conversation with the president, the hot line rings, and he just looks at it and decides not to answer it, giving you all his attention. The third man said, "You both have it wrong. Real status is when you are invited to the White House for a conversation with the president, the hot line rings, the president answers it and says, 'Here, it's for you'."

There is an amazing affirmation in the Book of First John: "See what love the Father has given us, that we should be called children of God; and so we are" (1 John 3:1). But we have not claimed our status as children if we continue to act like orphans.

It makes all the difference in the world whether you say, "Jesus is a savior" or "Jesus has saved me"; whether you say, "The Lord is a shepherd" or "The Lord is *my* shepherd"; it makes the difference between being saved or lost.

You may have already shifted gears in your mind from the Hebrew shepherd to Jesus, who made the astounding claim:

> I am the good shepherd; I know my own and my own know me. . . .
> My sheep hear my voice, and I know them, and they follow me; and I give them eternal life, and they shall never perish, and no one shall snatch them out of my hand.
>
> (John 10:14, 27-28)

No language or even music can reveal the full power and tenderness of those words. Yet, the fact remains; these words must be *appropriated* by each one of us.

I had the marvelous and challenging opportunity of chairing the Program Committee for the World Methodist Conference which met in Nairobi, Kenya, in 1986. The presence of the delegation from South Africa flavored that conference more than any other factor, more than any of the programs we planned.

That year, Abel and Freda Hendricks from South Africa received The Upper Room Citation, an esteemed recognition of outstanding world Christian leadership and witness. Janice Grana, the world editor of The Upper Room, and other staff were going to South Africa for the presentation and a great celebration. At the last minute they were denied visas, so the citation had to be presented late in Abel and Freda's church in Capetown by some folks who were allowed to get in.

Since Mrs. Grana couldn't go to South Africa, she had a small dinner in Nairobi honoring Abel and Freda to which my wife, Jerry, and I were invited.

She gave the Hendrickses the opportunity to invite a few of their close friends out of the South African delegation to the dinner. It was a marvelous evening marked by a deep spiritual energy, as we knew we were breaking bread with men and women who were in the same line of Christian martyrs as Stephen and others through the centuries.

Most of these Christians from South Africa had been in detention and/or prison; most of them had been in many times. One had spent three years in the prison on Robben Island—no rights, held at the caprice of a government that had institutionalized evil in the sin of apartheid, stripped of dignity as a human being. Rights that should belong to all people were denied to three-fourths of that nation's population.

Yet, there was a holy happiness among those people who had gathered at the dinner. You could feel it. It drew you to them. I think, more than ever before, I felt the deep meaning of the Beatitudes—Jesus' charter for the kingdom—especially that eighth one: "Blessed are those who are persecuted for righteousness' sake, for theirs is the kingdom of heaven" (Matt. 5:10).

I knew at that dinner that those South Africans, both black and white, had a vision and a possession of the kingdom that I only vaguely sensed.

Jerry and I sat at dinner with the wife of a prominent South African man. Her twenty-one-year-old daughter was in detention, and God only knew what was happening to her. Her nineteen-year-old son was in a Scotland university. She said he may never be able to return. If he were to come back he might well be killed. When her children were fourteen, sixteen, and eighteen, they were all in detention at one time.

Can you imagine, as a parent, how you would live with that? Your children are jailed, and you have no power to do anything about it, no legal appeal.

The woman said to us, "I used to wonder about the Holy Spirit, about the personal presence of God; it was all ideas, theology, religious words—but not any more. I know the Holy Spirit. God is real to me. We are humanly powerless in face of the evil system, but our power from God is greater than the system."

It is no wonder she could laugh, and she laughed a lot. Her eyes danced. There was an uncommon joy that you could feel just by sitting beside her and listening to her.

She was saying in it all, "The Lord is my shepherd."

We can learn from this woman, even though our lot will probably never be so painfully tragic.

Jesus will not be content to be just *a* shepherd, or even a *good* shepherd. He wants us to say of him: *"My* shepherd."

Oh, the glory of it: "The Lord is my shepherd."

He Restores My Soul

I've seen shepherds in the western part of our country, driving their sheep very much like cowboys drive cattle. But in the Middle East, it's different. I've seen them often in the Holy Land; the shepherd leads the flock, going ahead of the sheep. I remember how fascinating it was when I first went to the Holy Land: All along the road from Jerusalem down to the Dead Sea, we would often see a shepherd walking through what seemed to be such barren land with forty or fifty sheep following behind. The shepherd leads.

That's the phrase in the psalm that describes the work of the shepherd: "He leads me." How readily we say it, how easily it settles in our minds, how gently it lays upon our hearts.

> He makes me lie down in green pastures
> He leads me beside still waters;
>   he restores my soul.
>   (Psalm 23:2-3)

So the shepherd leads . . . seeking green pastures and still waters. For what purpose? To restore my soul.

That's the primary task of the shepherd—to find the green pasture and the springs of water that will sustain the life of his flock. That's also the work of God in our lives. Christ, the Good Shepherd, leads us to places and through experiences which "restore our soul."

He Leads in Paths of Righteousness

It would be pleasant to stay at this point for a while, the Good Shepherd giving us rest, refreshing our fainting powers, restoring our souls. We don't want to forget that. He does make us lie down in green pastures and leads us to still waters and restores our soul. But that rest and renewal is not to wallow in. Our midday breaks can be extended too long. There is another picture here of the shepherd leading, another aspect of the shepherd's care: "He leads me in paths of righteousness for his name's sake" (Psalm 23:3).

David, our psalmist, will not let us distort the picture. The purpose of repose and refreshment is to prepare us for tasks and marches and action. David knew, as you and I must learn, that we may prize too much the peaceful hours of communion and waive or ignore the imperative call to righteousness.

Keep a perspective about our faith journey. Following the shepherd will include those experiences of deep communion when we rest in the Lord, when we're enriched by the knowledge of God's presence. We may even from time to time experience a mystical binding to the Lord. But all this must lead to a deeper commitment to walk the paths of righteousness, to take greater risks in love.

Did you read how Ferdinand Marcos, one-time president of the Philippines, said that his religious devotion kept him from committing suicide? It's too bad it did not keep him from stealing his country blind and persecuting his opponents. His wife, Imelda, complained that the media coverage was only showing her extravagances and the luxury of the palace in Manila, and not showing the prayer room in the palace, which would prove how pious they were.

Our inward spirituality must manifest itself in outward holiness. Donald Shelby reminds us that "unless the ecstasy of God's indwelling presence becomes the agony of sacrifice and obedience—working for God's kingdom by going the second mile, turning the other cheek, fulfilling our moral imperatives, and serving the least and the lost—then our ecstasy is pure baloney, our piety is a rank form of idolatry, and our religious talk is mere rhetoric" (Shelby, "Ecstasy and Baloney," May 25, 1980).

One of the primary reasons I'm a United Methodist is because of the emphasis on social holiness. John Wesley, our father in the faith, passionately argued that there could be no holiness but social holiness . . . and that to turn Christianity into a solitary religion is to destroy it.

One of Wesley's last written words was a letter to William Wilberforce, who, almost a lone voice and an isolated force, waged a radical campaign against slavery. Wesley's letter, written only a few days before his death, was a last-breath challenge to Wilberforce to walk on in the paths of righteousness. Here is a part of that letter:

> Unless the Divine Power has raised you up to be as *Athanasius contra mundum,* I see not how you can go through your glorious enterprise in opposing that execrable villainy, which is the scandal of religion, of England, and of human nature. Unless God has raised you up for this very thing, you will be worn out by the opposition of men and devils. But if God be for you, who can be against you? Are all of them together stronger than God? O be not weary in well doing. Go on, in the name of God and in the power of his might, till even American slavery (the vilest that ever saw the sun) shall vanish away before it (Telford, Vol. VIII, p. 265).

The Latin words in the first sentence, *contra mundum*, mean "against the world." The shepherd leads us that way—*contra mundum*, against the world—in the path of righteousness, for his name's sake. And we must follow, even when it goes against the tide of popular public opinion, even when it appears unpatriotic, even when it puts us at odds with family and friends. Justice and peace in South Africa, Afghanistan, Nicaragua, and Poland; poverty and hunger, pornography, and unemployment in Memphis—these are issues along the paths of righteousness for our shepherd's name's sake.

The question is: Are we willing to be led?

I hear it over and over again: "I'm afraid of what the Lord may do with me and where he might lead me." Even when it is not spoken, I sense that fear boiling in the lives of people, paralyzing them in their discipleship. Why is it that we tend to associate God's will with being unpleasant and tough? We talk about discovering and doing God's will in the same tone and with the same reservation that I used to resist my mother's entreaty to take a dose of castor oil or black draught.

It may be tough to make some of those hard decisions about God's will. It will require discipline and discernment to stay in God's will. But the inner peace, the feelings of worthwhileness, the ease of conscience, and the assurance of God's good pleasure and eternal life will offset any price we think we have to pay.

Many years ago, King Edward II and his Queen Alexandra were out walking on the moors some distance from their summit palace at Windsor. Suddenly, the queen stumbled and seriously sprained her ankle. Night was just beginning to fall. She was in great pain and could stand on only one leg. Finally, by leaning on her husband and hobbling on the other leg, they were able to reach the home of a humble cottager who had already gone to bed. The king pounded on the door until someone from within cried, "Who's there?" The king shouted, "It is Edward. It is your king. Let me in." The man behind the door shouted back, "Enough of your pranks! Be off with you and let a man get his sleep!" The man tried to go back to sleep, but Edward continued pounding on the door. The cottager shouted, "I'll teach you to torment an honest man who

129

is trying to get his sleep." He rushed downstairs with a stick in his hand, ready to throw the intruder off the porch. Then in the dim light of his candle he saw that it was indeed his king! He gasped, stepped back, dropped to his knees and invited the king and queen to come in. Help was quickly summoned.

Years later, when the cottager had grown old and company would come over, he would relive that experience. He would tell of that wonderful night the king came to his humble home. He would rock back and forth before the fire, smoking his pipe, and in a voice touched with awe he would say, "And to think, I almost didn't let him in! I almost didn't let him in!" (Harding, March 23, 1986).

We are in the same danger. The shepherd wants to lead us. The question is, are we willing to be led?

Thou Preparest a Table Before Me

This lovely image of the shepherd is so gripping that few of us note that change of imagery that comes in verse 5:

Thou preparest a table before me
　　in the presence of my enemies;
thou anointest my head with oil
　　my cup overflows.
　　　　　　(Psalm 23:5)

Here the Lord becomes a *host*, and we are *guests* at his table. There are three leadings in the last two verses that help to explain the message taught by the image of the Lord as our host.

First, "Thou preparest a table before me in the presence of my enemies."

I see two suggestions here: *providence* and *protection*. Providence is a big word, a big idea. One of our problems is that our ideas about God are too small. The psalmist works on that. He seems to be saying of himself: "I am more than Jehovah's sheep; I am Jehovah's guest."

This is a part of what providence means—we are guests of God in a world that God created, and whose destiny God will ultimately determine.

"Thou preparest a table before me." There is an intimacy in sharing a meal. In Old Testament Judaism, to eat with a person was a deep act of identification and acceptance. That's the reason the Pharisees became so angry at Jesus for eating with publicans and sinners. Eating was not only a means of satisfying hunger but an experience of intimate, affectionate love.

That's what the Shepherd Lord, who has become our banquet host, offers: his providence, expressed in love and daily care. Will we believe it? We sit at the table of God's daily providence.

When we tend to take pride over what we have accomplished, we need to take a closer look at ourselves. When we're drifting further and further into that deadly pit of self-sufficiency, we need to draw ourselves back. Where would we be without God?

The very air we breathe, God gives. Our physical life is but a flickering light, completely dependent upon a remarkable intrastructure of life which God provides.

That's the reason I can't understand people who do not tithe. To neglect to tithe is like glaringly snubbing your nose at God. It is a gross stance of ingratitude and selfishness. Jesus made the point when he told the story of the successful farmer who tore down his barns and built bigger barns. You remember the story. God's judgment is graphic: "Fool! This night your soul is required of you." That has a frightening curtains-down ring to it. But the haunting line is the one that follows: "And the things you have prepared, whose will they be?" (Luke 12:20).

Let that question jangle your conscience when you begin to think about what *you* have done, what *you* have achieved, how successful and sufficient *you* are. Give that question your clearest consideration when you're deciding what part of your income you are going to give to the Lord. "And these things you have prepared, whose will they be?" These are not passing questions of the moment; they have to do with eternity. Where would you be? Whose would your things be if God's daily providence were withdrawn?

But there's another side to the coin. Peter captured it in his first epistle, chapter 5, verses 6 and 7:

> Humble yourselves therefore under the mighty hand of God, that in due time he may exalt you. Cast all your anxieties on him, for he cares about you.

What a promise—"Cast all your anxieties on him." This is our call to trust the loving providence of God.

I have a dear friend who has learned to trust God's providence, but oh, had he learned it earlier! What a difference there would be. He's about to get married for the third time. The failure of his earlier marriages witnesses to his self-centered efforts to control and determine destiny and his narrow focus on his own selfish desires. Now with a deep experience of God's grace and a commitment to the graceful providence of God, his whole thought process is changing.

His marriage is being delayed because of his fiancée's unwillingness to make the final commitment. My friend's current economic uncertainty is holding her back.

My friend asked me recently, "Do you believe the marriage vows, literally?"

"Literally!" I said.

"I never did before," he responded, "and that has been my problem. But now I know that it can't be any other way—a literal commitment 'for better, for worse; for richer, for poorer.'"

Then he went on to make the clearest Christian witness I've heard him make: "I've surrendered myself to the Lord—and that includes my economic life. I'm trusting God, and my happiness now is not dependent upon the success of this project." He was talking about a miltimillion dollar project that is an up-and-down proposition and could lead to bankruptcy. It had been a source of tension and anxiety.

My friend is at the right place now. Many of us need to join him there in response to the scripture in 1 Peter 5:6-7. We need to humbly cast all our anxieties on God, knowing God cares for us.

That's the first suggestion of the image of the table set before us. But, other than *providence*, there is *protection*—protection in the presence of our enemies: "Thou preparest a table before me in the presence of my enemies" (Psalm 23:5).

We talked about protection in chapter 3, but let's look at it again.

The Psalms are full of expressions of this bracing truth. Listen to some of them:

The Lord is a stronghold for the oppressed,
  a stronghold in times of trouble.
                              (Psalm 9:9)

I love thee, O Lord, my strength.
The Lord is my rock, and my fortress, and my deliverer,
  my God, my rock, in whom I take refuge.
                              (Psalm 18:1-2)

But thou, O Lord, art a shield about me,
  my glory, and the lifter of my head.
                              (Psalm 3:3)

It's a matter of trust and commitment—the Lord will protect us. The Lord will eat with us—be intimately present in the presence of our enemies, in the presence of those circumstances and forces that would lead us astray and take us far from the righteous path.

"Greater is he that is within you, than he that is in the world" (1 John 4:4, KJV). More and more I'm convinced that Satan and the powers of evil are after God's people every day. We must claim the protection of God—believing and acting on the fact that God will prepare a table before us in the presence of our enemies. We must call on God as we begin to sense the tempter's approach. We must immerse ourselves in God's word and in daily prayer so that we may be alive to the Lord's presence and know that providence and protection.

Thou Anointest My Head with Oil

Now another affirmation: "Thou anointest my head with oil, my cup overflows" (Psalm 23:5).

To see this picture clearly, we must watch the shepherd leading his sheep toward the sheepfold in the evening. They've been out all day in the barren, hostile, dangerous countryside. Their feet are tender, their knees are perhaps scraped by the rocks, and, in some cases, their heads are scratched by sharp thorns. Now it is sunset and the time for rest. The sheepfold is in sight.

At the end of the day, the shepherd, going in front of the sheep, would stand in the gateway and call the sheep to him. As they came he would examine them one by one. Sheep are peculiarly susceptible to fevers. The feet might need attention. The grazed head or torn knee would be treated with soothing oil (Weatherhead, pp. 162-163).

That's the way the shepherd anointed the sheep, caring for their wounds. It's a picture of sustaining grace—the ministering love of God. Returning to the image of our being a guest at the table of the Lord, the idea of anointing is also present, in the image of the Eastern feast in which guests are anointed with precious perfumes by the host, upon entering his home. It's a beautiful picture. When the psalmist says that God anoints him with oil, he is saying that God is like the host who always greets us in love. God gives generously to us and wants to meet our needs.

God confers upon us, not only necessities, but an extravagant grace that makes some of our darkest hours shine and puts a sweetness into our most bitter experience.

I've seen it happen, and I've experienced it myself—an extra portion of grace showered upon me unexpectedly. We see in this grace the anointing hand of God. We may know this anointing:

- In the midst of an illness;
- At a time when loving relationships are strained;
- When confusion darkens our lives and we are frozen in a place out of which we think we may never be delivered;
- In those circumstances we feel God's hand touching our lives, anointing us with the fragrance of God's presence. It is as if God is saying, "I'm here. Trust me. Lo, I am with you always."

Here is a picture of God's anointing in the area of our need for forgiveness. Kenyon Scudder, the distinguished penologist, told a story of a friend of his who was riding one day on a train. Seated next to him was a troubled young man. Finally, the young man blurted out that he was a convict returning from prison. His crime had brought shame on his family. They had written to him, but he had refused to respond or to see them because he was so ashamed for what he had done. Now he was out of prison, headed back home.

He wanted to make it easy for his family to let him know if they didn't want him to come home, so he had written them to put up a signal when the train passed their farm on the outskirts of town. If they wanted him to return home, they were to tie a white ribbon on the apple tree near the tracks. If they did not want him back, they were to do nothing, and he would stay on the train and go West and lose himself forever.

Nearing his hometown, the young man's suspense and discomfort grew to the point that he could not bear to look at the tree. Scudder's friend offered to watch, and the two exchanged places by the train window. The young man buried his face in his hands. A few minutes later, the friend laid his hand on the young man's shoulder and whispered in a broken voice, "It's all right! The whole tree is white with ribbons!"

That's the extravagance of God's grace—we receive *more* than what we need. This is true not only with forgiveness, but with all God's ministering love. "Thou anointest my head with oil; *my cup overflows.*"

I Shall Dwell in the House of the Lord

And now that final, climactic, triumphant word:

> Surely goodness and mercy shall follow me
>   all the days of my life;
> and I shall dwell in the house of the Lord
>   for ever.
>
> (Psalm 23:6)

There are two ways of looking at this verse, both providing vital lessons.

One is to go back and pick up the image of the shepherd and the sheepfold, and to link it with that incomparable word in John 10, verse 9: "I am the door; if any one enters by me, he will be saved, and will go in and out and find pasture."

Verse 6 is the picture of our being with the shepherd and belonging to his flock. James Moffatt translates the phrase "in the house of the Lord forever" as "within his household evermore." That means *belonging* to the flock—belonging to the family.

Knowing that we are a part of God's forever family, we can move through life with courage and joy. There may be mountains of trouble and turmoil over which we will have to climb. Swamps of despondency and despair may pull us under, drowning our spiritual sensitivity and blinding us to the light of God's presence. Certainly we will pass through the valley of the shadow of death. Yet, the knowledge of belonging to the family—being within the Lord's household forevermore—will provide us with the bracing and energizing power to carry on. Because we have entered into the household by the way of the Good Shepherd, we know we are saved, and we can rise every morning and face a new day in the pasture of our lives.

We can also look at this verse from the perspective of the Lord being our host. The Lord will bring us at last to his glorious home, where we will be honored guests forevermore.

Heaven. "In my Father's house are many mansions" (John 14:2, KJV). Here is the promise of the soul's true home. And there is magic in that word *home*. There is power in that word.

> It will draw the wanderer from the ends of the earth. It will nerve sailor, and soldier, and explorer to heroic endurance. It will melt with its dear memories the hardened criminal. It will bring a film of tears over the eyes of the man of the world. What will not a charwoman do or bear if only she can keep her little home together? (Meyer, pp. 141-142).

Glory! The Lord is *my* shepherd. The Lord is also my host who prepares a table in the presence of my enemies. I can trust the providence and protection of the Lord. My Lord anoints my head with oil, with extravagant grace that is more than sufficient. My Lord brings me at last to the eternal home where I will dwell forevermore. Glory!

STUDY QUESTIONS FOR

PERSONAL REFLECTION AND GROUP DISCUSSION

CHAPTER ONE: O TASTE AND SEE

For Personal Reflection

1. What is your favorite psalm? Reflect upon your experience with this psalm. Why does it have such meaning for you?

2. Have there been many experiences in your life when you put your security in the wrong place? Reflect on the result of this.

3. Recall and reflect upon an experience when you came to *know* God, because you first came to know your need of God.

4. Is it a new notion for you that your relationship to God is not only of value to you, it is of value to God? Ponder that truth and *enjoy* the affirmation it brings.

5. What are you experiencing now that you could live with more meaningfully if you could claim the promise: "Weeping may tarry for the night, but joy comes with the morning"?

For Group Discussion

1. Invite persons to share their favorite psalms and tell why those psalms have special meaning.

2. Talk about what it means to *presume* on God's grace.

3. How does self-sufficiency prevent us from experiencing God's grace?

4. Discuss knowing our need of God as a condition for knowing God.

5. Invite two or three persons to share what they felt when they came to realize that their relationship to God was not only of value to them but of value to God.

6. Allow persons who wish to share a present situation with which they might deal more meaningfully if they could claim the promise: "Weeping may tarry for the night, but joy comes with the morning.

7. Close your discussion by inviting the group to share any comments or questions they have on this chapter.

CHAPTER TWO: WHEN YOU FEEL TRAPPED

For Personal Reflection

1. Is there an area of your life or a relationship in your life in which you feel trapped? Think about it and try to determine *why* you feel this way. Who and/or what determines your bondage?

2. Is there a situation from which you want desperately to run away?

3. Is there a problem in your life that you have not shared honestly with God or asked for help because you have not been willing to acknowledge it and face it honestly?

4. Recall your most vivid experience of God at work in your life in a particular way. Are there aspects of that experience, that if you put into practice every day, would enhance your ongoing experience of God?

For Group Discussion

1. Begin your discussion with persons sharing the most meaningful insight from this chapter.

2. Invite group members to share an experience when they felt trapped—and how they overcame those feelings.

3. Are there persons who would like to share present experiences of feeling trapped?

4. Discuss the three truths listed on pages 36-37 about facing our problems honestly.

5. Spend a few minutes talking about what it means to *conference* with yourself as a dimension of prayer.

6. Let two persons share an experience when God has worked in their life in a particular way. Then discuss whether there are aspects of those experiences that if put into practice would enhance your ongoing experience of God.

CHAPTER THREE: A CONFIDENCE FOR ALL SEASONS

For Personal Reflection

1. In your life, *right now,* are you "borrowing trouble"? fearing something that *may* be?

2. Is there a fear in your life that you have not allowed the Lord to help you manage?

3. Is there some area of your life where you feel a need for protection?

4. Recall and reflect upon your most recent experience of God being "far off."

5. Is there something going on in your life now about which you might receive insight and relief if you would share it with a pastor or a trusted friend?

6. Have there been times in your life when God seemed absent, yet your faith grew?

For Group Discussion

1. Invite persons in the group to share experiences of "borrowing trouble"—fearing what might have been, but never was.

2. Talk for a few minutes about how fear immobilizes us.

3. Discuss how we can keep our fears manageable.

4. How do people you know talk about God's protection? How do you perceive it? Is there any new insight in the discussion of protection in this chapter?

5. Discuss Spurgeon's word, "It is not the trouble, but the hiding of our Father's face, which cuts us to the quick."

6. Discuss the notion that sharing our feelings and problems with others may be the dynamic that will enable us to share honestly with God. Also, the opposite—sharing with God frees us to share with others.

7. Talk about our feelings of God's absence being occasions for growth in faith.

CHAPTER FOUR: PUT THOU MY TEARS IN THY BOTTLE

For Personal Reflection

1. Can you recall an experience when, though you didn't use the words, you prayed to God to, "put thou my tears in thy bottle"?

2. Recall some suffering in your life that was not wasted; something that brought meaning to you or someone else.

3. Do you need to claim the confidence of the psalmist, "This I know, that God is for me"? What change of attitude would come if you really believed that?

4. Recall and reflect upon how your trust in God has been tested by pain and suffering.

5. Can you recall persons, such as Dr. Beaty, who have been able to live gratefully and graciously, though burdened by sorrow, pain, or trouble? What is the big lesson you can learn from them?

For Group Discussion

1. Spend a few minutes sharing the new insights that have come to persons in the group from studying this chapter.

2. Invite two or three persons to share some suffering that was not wasted, that brought meaning either to their lives or to someone else's.

3. Is there a person in the group whose attitude toward a particular situation, relationship, or problem would change if they could accept in confidence the word of the psalmist, "This I know, that God is for me"?

4. Discuss the problems and limitations of turning to the Lord only in times of calamity.

5. Invite persons to share how their trust in God has been tested by pain and suffering.

6. Discuss gratitude and knowing the source of blessing in the context of pain and suffering.

CHAPTER FIVE:
SINGING THE LORD'S SONG IN A FOREIGN LAND

For Personal Reflection

1. What is the most pronounced conflict you have with images of God in the Bible? Have these conflicts caused you to question the Bible? Have they affected your faith in any way?

2. What is the "foreign land" in which you currently find yourself that calls for a reexamination and a renewal of your faith?

3. Recall and reflect upon your most recent experience when you could not sing "the Lord's song."

4. Who have been two or three persons who have helped you sing the Lord's song when you couldn't sing it by yourself?

5. Think about a person or persons who need someone to sing the Lord's song with them. How might you do that?

For Group Discussion

1. Discuss the images of growth and journey as models for the Christian life.

2. Review the five suggestions about how we look at the Bible. Which of these offers new meaning for you? Why?

3. Discuss the "foreign lands" in which we are living today that call for a reexamination and a renewal of our understanding and experience of faith?

4. Invite any who will to share their most recent experiences of being unable to sing the Lord's song.

5. Spend some time sharing about persons who have helped you sing the Lord's song. What did they do? How did they relate to you? What was it that enabled you to sing again?

CHAPTER SIX: HOW MAY WE COME TO GOD?

For Personal Reflection

1. Spend five minutes thinking about God. Just focus on who God is and how you experience God in your life.

2. What are some areas in your life where you act as though you were "king" rather than God being sovereign in your life?

3. What is your favorite title for God? Why?

4. Do your attitudes (pure heart) sometimes conflict with your actions (clean hands)? How do you resolve this?

5. What is there in your life that speaks clearly to the fact that your hands are not clean and your heart is not pure?

6. In what area of your life do you most need to relinquish command? How might you begin to do this?

7. Is there a burden you are carrying that could be made lighter by acknowledging that you don't have to carry it alone?

8. What is the barrier that prevents you from *resting*, from making "the pause" a part of the rhythm of your life?

For Group Discussion

1. Spend some time discussing what terms like "Lord of Hosts," "King of Glory," "Sovereign Lord" suggest to you.

2. Let each person in the group share her/his favorite title for God. If there is a reason, in two or three sentences, tell why this image is so meaningful.

3. Can persons have pure hearts and unclean hands? Clean hands without a pure heart? If the two, attitude and action, are in conflict, how do we resolve the issue?

4. Discuss the difference between sincerity of purpose and success of performance.

5. What does it mean to say that being with God is a matter of will and willingness?

6. Invite persons in the group to share their own experience of seeking to carry "the whole world" in their minds and on their hearts.

7. What are the barriers preventing you from "resting," from making "the pause" a part of the rhythm of your life?

8. Was there something you would have talked about, some area of concern you would have discussed had you been writing a chapter on these two psalms (24 and 127)?

CHAPTER SEVEN:
IN THE HOUSE OF THE LORD FOREVER

For Personal Reflection

1. Recall your earliest recollection of hearing the Twenty-Third Psalm, the setting, and what it meant to you.

2. Recall and reflect upon the occasion when the Twenty-Third Psalm was most meaningful as a source of strength, guidance, and comfort.

3. In response to chapter 6 you were asked to reflect upon your favorite image or title of God. What about *shepherd?* How do you feel about that image?

4. Examine your prayer life. Do you find yourself trying to convince the Lord to be your shepherd, or do you accept the fact that God is your shepherd and rejoice in it? Do you practice the positive element of praying, as discussed in Leslie Weatherhead's quote on page 123, rather than concentrating on petitions that emphasize the negative?

5. Recall and reflect upon the specific occasion or the time frame in your life when you became conscious of the fact that "the Lord is *my* Shepherd"—a personal relationship with God.

6. Is there a call upon your life now to follow the Shepherd in "paths of righteousness"—to leave the green pastures and still waters of repose and renewal for action and involvement?

7. Have you known an experience when the Lord has prepared a table before you "in the presence of my enemies"? Reflect on that experience. What does it teach you about daily living?

For Group Discussion

1. Invite as many as will to share their most meaningful experience with the Twenty-Third Psalm.

2. Discuss William Temple's statement: "If your conception of God is radically false, then the more devout you are, the worse it will be for you."

3. Discuss the difference between positive affirmation in prayer and petition that emphasizes the negative. Share personally your style of praying and whether this is a new idea.

4. Invite two or three persons to share the specific occasion or time frame when they began to consciously claim that "the Lord is *my* Shepherd"—a personal relationship with God.

5. Discuss the notion of the Shepherd leading us in "paths of righteousness"—calling us from the "green pastures" of repose and renewal to action and involvement.

6. What would it mean if the congregation of which you are a part would sense the Divine Power raising it up *contra mundum,* against the world?

7. Invite as many as will to share experiences when they have received an extra portion of grace—when the Lord has "anointed my head with oil."

8. What is the most meaningful truth you have learned from this study of the psalms?

NOTES

Sources quoted in this book are identified in the text by author and page number. If more than one work by the same author is cited, the title of the work is included in the citation. Bibliographic information for each source is listed below.

Allen, W. Loyd. *Crossroads in Christian Growth*. Nashville: Broadman Press, 1989.

Beaty, Dr. Harold. "Life's Greatest Virtue" (unpublished sermon), December 30, 1979.

Boulware, Barry. "The Power Is Not Yours" (unpublished sermon), February 16, 1986.

Buchwald, Art. "No money, no product, no service, no mercy" in *The Commercial Appeal*, Memphis, Tenn., March 8, 1986.

Campbell, Ernest T. "The Gift of Sleep" (unpublished sermon), March 5, 1972. "The Lord's Song in a Strange Land" (unpublished sermon), April 30, 1972.

Cassidy, Sheila. *Audacity to Believe*. Cleveland: Collins World, 1978.

Chappell, Clovis G. *Sermons from the Psalms*. Nashville: Abingdon-Cokesbury Press, 1931.

Coffin, William Sloane. *The Courage to Love*. San Francisco: Harper & Row, Publishers, 1982.

Craghan, John F. *The Psalms*. Wilmington: Michael Glazier, Inc., 1985.

Fosdick, Henry Emerson. "The Meaning of Prayer," quoted in *A Guide to Prayer for Ministers and Other Servants*. Nashville: The Upper Room, 1983.

Hamilton, J. Wallace. *Where Now Is Thy God?* Old Tappan: Fleming A. Revell Company, 1969.

Harding, Joe A. "The Power of Passionate Purpose!" (unpublished sermon), March 23, 1986.

Hubbard, David Allan. *More Psalms for All Seasons*. Grand Rapids: Wm. B. Eerdmans, 1975.

King, Martin Luther, Jr. *Strength to Love*. New York: Harper & Row, 1963.

Kirkpatrick, Dow. "The Cross of Snow" (unpublished sermon), January 28, 1968.

Kunkel, Fritz. *In Search of Maturity*. New York: Charles Scribner's Sons, 1948.

Meyer, F. B. *The Shepherd Psalm*. London: Morgan & Scott, n.d.

Moltmann, Jurgen. *The Power of the Powerless*. San Francisco: Harper & Row, 1983.

Naylor, Gloria. *The Women of Brewster Place*. New York: Penguin Books, 1980.

Patchen, Kenneth. "Blood of the Sun" in *The Collected Poems of Kenneth Patchen*. New York: New Directions, 1968.

Sclater, J.R.P. *The Interpreter's Bible*, volume 4. Nashville: Abingdon Press, 1955.

Shelby, Donald. "True Security" (unpublished sermon), March 19, 1985. Quote from "Listening to the Left Hand," in *Harper's*, December, 1973, p. 92. "How Deep Is Down?" (unpublished sermon), February 25, 1983. Quote from "Dying is More Beautiful the Second Time Around," *Honolulu Star-Bulletin*, July 26, 1971. "Ecstasy and Baloney" (unpublished sermon), May 25, 1980.

Spurgeon, C.H. *The Treasury of David*, Vol. 1. Hendrickson, Mass.: Hendrickson Publishers, Inc., 1988.

Telford, John (editor). *The Letters of the Rev. John Wesley, A.M.* London: The Epworth Press, 1931.

Temple, William. *Daily Readings* by William Temple. Nashville: Abingdon Press, 1965. Compiled by Hugh C. Warner, edited by William Wand.

Walker, Alice. *The Color Purple.* New York: Pocket Books, 1982.

Weatherhead, Leslie D. *A Shepherd Remembers.* London: Hodder and Stoughton, 1937/1960.